Matthias Kirsch

Brand Equity in the Banking Industry

D1808366

Matthias Kirsch

Brand Equity in the Banking Industry

What are the Determinants of Brand Equity in the Banking Industry?

Social Sciences Series

Impressum / Imprint

Bibliografische Information der Deutschen Nationalbibliothek: Die Deutsche Nationalbibliothek verzeichnet diese Publikation in der Deutschen Nationalbibliografie; detaillierte bibliografische Daten sind im Internet über http://dnb.d-nb.de abrufbar.
Alle in diesem Buch genannten Marken und Produktnamen unterliegen warenzeichen-, marken- oder patentrechtlichem Schutz bzw. sind Warenzeichen oder eingetragene Warenzeichen der jeweiligen Inhaber. Die Wiedergabe von Marken, Produktnamen, Gebrauchsnamen, Handelsnamen, Warenbezeichnungen u.s.w. in diesem Werk berechtigt auch ohne besondere Kennzeichnung nicht zu der Annahme, dass solche Namen im Sinne der Warenzeichen- und Markenschutzgesetzgebung als frei zu betrachten wären und daher von jedermann benutzt werden dürften.

Bibliographic information published by the Deutsche Nationalbibliothek: The Deutsche Nationalbibliothek lists this publication in the Deutsche Nationalbibliografie; detailed bibliographic data are available in the Internet at http://dnb.d-nb.de.
Any brand names and product names mentioned in this book are subject to trademark, brand or patent protection and are trademarks or registered trademarks of their respective holders. The use of brand names, product names, common names, trade names, product descriptions etc. even without a particular marking in this works is in no way to be construed to mean that such names may be regarded as unrestricted in respect of trademark and brand protection legislation and could thus be used by anyone.

Coverbild / Cover image: www.ingimage.com

Verlag / Publisher:
AV Akademikerverlag GmbH & Co. KG
Heinrich-Böcking-Str. 6-8, 66121 Saarbrücken, Deutschland / Germany
Email: info@akademikerverlag.de

Herstellung: siehe letzte Seite /
Printed at: see last page
ISBN: 978-3-639-45886-2

Table of Contents

List of Figures

List of Tables

Abstract

The following research paper examines the applicability of a customer-based brand equity model, based on Aakers' well-known brand equity dimensions, in order to determine the most relevant brand value drivers. This study was conducted in the banking industry. The findings reveal brand loyalty and perceived quality and service in connection with customer satisfaction to be the most influencing factors of brand equity in the retail banking market. Brand awareness and brand associations possess almost no explanatory power. The findings might help practitioners when developing new strategic marketing actions and expands the picture of the currently under-researched literature concerning brand equity in the service industry. The paper further formulates several propositions about possible differences of brand equity depending on tangible or intangible product related industries.

1 Introduction

1.1 General Introduction and Research Motivation

The concept of brand equity has received much attention by academics and practitioners in the last decades, as the brand is considered to be one of the most valuable assets within a company being responsible for obtaining and sustaining a competitive advantage (Ailawadi, Lehmann, & Neslin, 2003). A competitive advantage is very important, specifically in a highly competitive and homogenous marketplace as the retail banking sector. The value of intangible assets, especially the brand value, is difficult to measure objectively. A standardized approach of calculating brand equity does not exist; in fact there are plenty of different methods delivering divergent results (Trommsdorff, 2004). Neither does a standardized definition exist, nor a common concept of the main influencing factors of brand equity.

Brand equity can be viewed from different perspectives (Keller, 1993). One perspective is the financial approach, where "brand equity is defined as the incremental cash flows which accrue to branded products over unbranded products." (Simon & Sullivan, 1993, p. 28). Those monetary calculations can serve accounting purposes, merger and acquisitions, divestiture purposes, etc. (Keller, 1993). Another perspective is the behavioral approach, where "brand equity can be estimated by subtracting the utility of physical attributes of the product from the total utility of a brand." (Yoo, Donthu, & Lee, 2000, p. 195). The behavioral approach focuses on brand strategies necessary to develop points of difference to create a competitive advantage over unbranded products (Aaker, 1991). Although plenty of research exists to support both perspectives, it is easy to manifest a lack of standardization in the valuation and definition of brand equity. Companies lose trust in existing methods as a survey of Kriegbaum (2001) shows: Only 37.2% of the companies implemented a brand equity valuation method. 36.7% criticize explicitly the lack of applicable approaches. A measurement tool for brand equity is necessary and helps several processes: it helps the marketing decision making process, assesses the extendibility of a brand, tracks the brand's health compared to competitors and might assist within financial transactions (Ailawadi, Lehmann, & Neslin, 2003).

Nonetheless, brand equity develops a different character and meaning depending on the industry sector: most brand equity literature is "biased towards products" (Mackay, 2001, p. 210); the importance of brand equity in the service sector is still under-researched (Chang et al., 2008; Krishnan & Hartline, 2001). Vargo and Lusch (2008) underline the importance of the service coming along with the product and being an essential factor of success. Specifically in industries with a rather homogeneous product landscape, as the retail banking market, the service quality becomes a crucial thing in order to be successful and to be distinguishable from competitors. In the product industry there exists typically a variety of brands for different products and different customer segments (from luxury brands to basic and cheap brands); the product becomes the primary brand; in the service sector, however, the company itself becomes the primary brand (Berry, 2000). Therefore the brand carries a significant importance for the company as every brand dilution will have negative effects for the whole company. In this context brands help "to better visualize and understand intangible products" (Berry, 2000, p. 128) and to reduce perceived risk resulting from possible customer brand changes (Chang et al., 2008).

1.2 Brand Equity in the Retail Banking Industry

My thesis investigates the impact of certain brand dimensions on brand equity in the retail banking market. The retail banking market is a very interesting industry for analysis because it is a "highly competitive, complex and dynamic environment" and comprises financial products as well as financial services (Beerli, Martín, & Quintana, 2004, p. 253). The differentiation of products and services is at a rather low level (Ivanauskiene & Auruskeviciene, 2009). As a result brand equity dimensions as service quality or brand loyalty are crucial factors of success and an attractive area for research (Siddiqi, 2011). Specifically, there is a lack of research concerning service quality, customer satisfaction and loyalty in the retail banking industry (Cengiz, Ayyildiz, & Er, 2007).

This study uses Aakers' (1991, 1996) proposed brand equity dimensions, as it is the most cited and established consumer brand perception model in literature (Low & Lamb, 2000). The model follows Yoo's et al. (2000, p. 207) research proposition who call "the interaction effect of brand equity dimensions on brand equity" a very important future research issue. The understanding of brand equity in a service dominant sector is strengthened, as the majority of brand equity literature is concerned with tangible products (Krishnan & Hartline, 2001). It remains questionable whether the same brand equity dimensions hold for products and services. Practitioners and academics support such a difference in brand equity within the industries, nevertheless, there is rather less academic material concerning the service sector (Mackay, 2001). It is further of high interest whether brand equity in the banking sector is comparable to the findings of existing (product related) literature.

1.3 Problem Definition

1.3.1 Problem Statement

Based on extensive literature a model is designed to test different brand equity dimensions in the retail banking industry.

The central focus of investigation is the question:
What are the determinants of brand equity in the banking industry?

1.3.2 Research Questions

Following the central problem statement various sub questions arise:

What is brand value and what are its dimensions?

This question is the starting point of the thesis, as the literature review gives a broad overview of the topic. The miscellaneousness of brand equity is reviewed and various research directions are paid attention to.

What are the main value drivers of brand equity in the service related banking industry?

This question deals with the specific problem that brand equity dimensions might be different among different industries. Aakers' dimensions (1991, 1996) are used to distinguish between the central value drivers of brand equity in the banking industry.

What are the differences to other (product related) industries?

Since most of the brand equity literature is concerned with product related brands, I want to show communalities and differences of certain brand equity dimensions to the service sector.

1.3.3 Contribution

The findings of this study contribute to a better understanding of brand equity and its determinants in the service sector, specifically in the retail banking market. The study shows the differences between the most important value drivers of product related brands and service (banking) brands. In the service sector brand associations or awareness aspects have a minor importance. Customer satisfaction and perceived quality in connection with brand loyalty form the most important value drivers. The results not only add value to the theoretical research, but also support managers in the strategic decision making process.

1.4 Outline

The second chapter *Literature Review* introduces into the overall topic brand value. It gives a broad overview over current brand and brand equity definitions. Additionally, brand equity valuation methods are presented. Next, the research methodology is described. Following the analytical framework, a questionnaire is designed in order to test the brand dimensions. The next chapter presents the pure statistical results of the study. The *Discussion* part analyses and interprets the results. The last chapter summarizes the outputs, gives theoretical and managerial implications, shows limitations of this study and proposes future research opportunities.

2 Literature Review

2.1 The Role of a Brand

Practitioners and academics have been paying increasing attention to the concept of brand equity, as brands can be a source for the competitive advantage (Ailawadi, Lehmann, & Neslin, 2003). Firms realize that brand names might be one of the most valuable assets within the company and strengthening its position will be a top management priority (Goldfarb, Lu, & Moorthy, 2009; Keller & Sood, 2003; Kim, Kim & An, 2003; Neal & Strauss, 2008). Barth et al. (1998) show that "brand value estimates are significantly associated with equity market values" and should be a relevant and reliable part of equity valuations. Interbrand[1] publishes a yearly ranking of the worlds most valuable brands. In the 2009 ranking (Interbrand, 2010) first seated Coca Cola was assigned a brand value of 68.734 million USD which was about 34 % of the total market capitalzation at the end of 2009. Second seated IBM had a brand value of 60.211 million USD which was about 21 % of the toal market capitalzation. To underline the importance of brands, Interbrand has shown that stronger brands not only deliver greater stock

---

[1] Interbrand was founded in 1974 and is the world's biggest brand consultancy. Interbrand developed a method of valuing brands in monetary terms.

returns within a benchmark portfolio, but also at a lower risk (Madden, Fehle, & Fournier, 2006). Strong brands can generate a variaty of associations that help the customer to decide and are beyond the objective product value (Keller & Lehmann, 2006). New products can be launched at significantly lower costs through the presence of a strong brand (Keller & Sood, 2003). It can secure a stability of future sales (Kapferer, 2008) and give pricing power to the firm (Goldfarb, Lu, & Moorthy, 2009).

What is a brand and what are its dimensions? Kapferer (2008) claims that an internationally agreed legal definition does not exist. He suggests the following definition: "a sign or set of signs certifying the origin of a product or service and differentiating it from the competition" (Kapferer, 2008, p. 10). However, the *German Trade Act* law offers a broad and extensive legal definition: "Any signs, particularly words, including personal names, designs, letters, numerals, sound marks, three-dimensional configurations, including the shape of distinguishing the goods or services of one undertaking from those of other undertakings may be protected as trade marks" (Markengesetz, 2010). The legal purpose of brands is to distinguish one product or service from another by marking it with a unique sign.

Brands mean different things to different people. Actually there are many different definitions proposed by many academics. Neal & Strauss (2008) point out that it depends on the viewpoint of a person what a brand could mean to him: The employee might have a different opinion than the consumer. For employees a brand might provide identity, community and opportunity. The provider sees the possible competitive advantage a brand can create. The investor is mostly interested in the additional future cash flow generated by the brand. A brand can create a basis for cooperation and understanding for channel partners. The top management might use a brand as a motivational tool, etc. Nevertheless, "brands manifest their impact at three primary levels – customer market, product market, and financial market" (Keller & Lehmann, 2006, p. 740). The literature review will focus on these three levels and I will define these levels further.

Customer viewpoint

David Ogilvy[2] defined a brand 1951 as "the consumer's idea of a product". Aaker (1991) gives a comprehensive definition of a brand: "A set of brand assets and liabilities linked to a brand, its name and symbol, that adds to or detracts from the value provided by a product or service to a firm and/or to the firm's customers". Later further definitions which focus on the consumer as the central point within the brand, have been evoked. "A brand is a set of mental associations, held by the consumer which add to the perceived value of a product or service" (Keller, 1998, p. 13). Keller emphasizes the "differential effect" that arises from differences in consumer reactions. Without those differences the product could just be classified as commodity (Keller, 2008). Brand knowledge about the brand can build differences leading to a positive or negative choice for one or another product and is highly influenced by marketing activities (Keller, 2008). Kapferer (2008) points out the effect of a brand on the consumer by saying "a brand is a name that influences buyers". Most importantly is that brand equity can be built upon attributes that own no actual value (Broniarczyk & Gershoff, 2003).

Company viewpoint

From a company's perspective a brand can be the most valuable asset. Strong brands can lead to a variety of advantages for the company resulting in an additional cash flow (Kapferer, 2008). Hoeffler and Keller (2003) show empirically advantages of strong brands on consumer based brand equity. Strong brands are supposed to have "memory encoding and storage

---

[2] David Ogilvy (1911-1999) was an advertising execute. He founded the famous advertising agency "Ogilvy & Mather".

advantage over unknown brands in building brand awareness and image" (Hoeffler & Keller, 2003, p. 423). Consumers will have stronger links in mind and pay more attention to familiar brands because typically familiar brands have successfully developed consumer knowledge structures (Kent & Allen, 1994). With a greater number of associations those brands are more likely to be chosen for purchase (Lehmann & Pan, 1994). Being loss averse, switching costs for using an unknown brand loom larger for strong brands which leads to a higher price paid (Dhar & Simonson, 1992). Additionally, there might occur indirect favorable associations with stronger brands (Hoch & Deighton, 1989). Hoeffler and Keller (2003) list various advantages in terms of marketing activity for stronger brands:[3] Familiarity with a brand can lead to an increased purchase intention of the products. Brand extensions of an established brand may be more efficient than those of an unknown brand. In terms of pricing, brand leaders can command higher prices and can better handle price increases (Simon, 1979; Sivakumar & Raj, 1997). On the communications level, advertisements of familiar brands seem to be more effective than for unknown brands. Consumers are even more likely to have negative reactions to repetitions of advertisements of unknown brands than for familiar brands (Campbell & Keller, 2003). In terms of channel-related marketing products of strong brands are more likely to be accepted and gain shelf space in e. g. supermarkets (Montgomery, 1975). Brands and their related marketing activities can build a certain image of a product and its quality in the minds of consumers that might not reflect reality and thus lead to purchases because of positive brand associations. Strong brands can exploit those inefficiencies and as a result generate extra cash flows (Erdem & Swait, 1998).

---

[3] See Hoeffler & Keller, 2003 p. 426-437 for a detailed view

Investor viewpoint

A brand can also be seen from the investor's viewpoint. Following this direction a brand is defined as "the incremental cash flows which accrue to branded products over unbranded products" (Simon & Sullivan, 1993, p. 28). Brands are seen as assets that are being sold and bought like plants and equipment (Keller & Lehmann, 2006). Specifically in the context of mergers and acquisitions brands convey a huge value. According to a survey of Pricewaterhouse Coopers and Sattler (2001) the brand value can be up to 62% of the total company value. Many companies consider buying other brands instead of lunching or extending brands of their own portfolio due to rising costs and failure risks (Mahajan, Rao, & Srivastava, 1994). Although the price paid for the intangible asset is reasonably high, the companies gain well-known brands with an immediate access to the (new) market. According to Mahajan et al. (1994) the benefits from taking over a brand are an enhanced performance and marketing efficiency, longevity of the brand and carryover potential to other brands. Barth et al. (1998) show the importance and impact of brand values on equity values. Therefore a monetary valuation of brand equity is of huge importance, although it seems to be very difficult if not impossible to develop a valid and comprehensible valuation method (Sattler, Högl, & Hupp, 2002).

2.2 Brand Dimensions

An important aspect of brand equity is how the value of a brand is built. Since originally the customer decides about this value by choosing one brand over the other generating revenue for the company, I will look at brand attributes or elements that determine value for the brand. In practice as well as in the literature there is a debate on what are the value drivers and several concepts have developed (Sattler, 2005). The basic and most important dimension is knowledge because without any memory consumers will not buy a brand (Alba, Hutchinson, & Lynch, 1991). If a consumer thinks of a specific brand, associations to e. g. its taste or advertisements are supposed to come to his mind. This study uses Aaker's (1991, 1996) proposed model to explain brand equity in the retail banking market: Aaker (1996) developed a set of brand equity measures "that could be applied across markets and products" (Aaker, 1996, p. 103). He called it "the brand equity ten". His measures should reflect brand equity and should not easily been copied. They should be close to the market and adapt to changes. Naturally, they must apply across brands and products. The brand equity ten are grouped into four categories of customer perceptions (namely loyalty, perceived quality/leadership, associations, awareness) and one category called market behavior. Loyalty is the core dimension of brand equity and contains the two measures price premium and customer satisfaction. Only a loyal customer will pay a price premium in comparison to other brands. Customer satisfaction refers to customers that are already using the product or service and might habitually buy the product or service. The next category contains the two measures perceived quality and leadership. Perceived quality is a key dimension for brand equity, as it is associated with price premiums, price elasticities, brand usage and even stock returns. The second measure leadership accounts for the dynamics in the market. Aspects like leading brands, innovation and popularity are part of the measurement. The next category *associations* can be built around three perspectives "brand as product (value), brand as person (brand personality) and the brand as organization (organizational associations)" (Aaker, 1996, p. 111). However, it is essential that these three measures contribute to a differentiation of the brand from others. Only if the brand is perceived to be different, it can generate e. g. price premiums. The next category contains awareness measures. Awareness is an important aspect for brands, as it can affect perceptions and attitudes. Levels of awareness can be recognition, top-of-mind, recall, etc. The last category market behavior reflects market measures. It contains market share and market price/distribution coverage.

Market share is a performance indicator of the brand and is easily available. However, market share can be affected by marketing actions like promotions, so the second measure relative market price should cover this aspect. It shows the relation of prices of the specific brand to all other brands in a specific product category.

Table 1: Summary of alternative viewpoints about brand equity dimensions

Authors	Main objective	Comparison to Aaker
Keller (2008)	Brand awareness and brand image as main value drivers. Brand awareness is the consumer's ability to remember and name a specific brand, when being confronted with the pure product the company makes. Brand image is defined as "perceptions about a brand as reflected by the brand associations held in consumer memory" (Keller, 1993, p. 3). Unique associations are important to show differentiations to competitors (unique selling point).	Aaker's model is more extensive. Keller's brand image is similar to Aakers' brand associations.

Neal & Strauss (2008)	Brand is defined as a contract, consumers are willing to accept in order to reduce the level of uncertainty. Two major components of brand equity: trust attributes and image attributes. Both depend on the product and the industry.	Image attributes relate to Aakers' brand associations. Trust attributes are different to Aaker's model.
Esch (2003)	Brand awareness and brand image as main value drivers. Awareness is the most important factor, since brands must be familiar in order to be (re-)purchased.	Similar to Keller (2008).
Sattler (1997, 2005)	Main value drivers (ordered to importance): brand image, historical performance, market share, repurchase rate, distribution, awareness.	Sattler includes financial measures. Awareness has not that high importance as in other models.

In summary, I conclude that Aaker's model is most useful in the retail banking industry, as it is the most extensive model applicable "across markets and products" (Aaker, 1996, p. 103). I select Aakers' proposed dimensions of brand equity as basic model because it is (1) the most cited consumer brand perception model in literature; (2) delivers established, reliable and published measures and (3) the dimensions are frequently discussed in recent literature[4] (Low & Lamb, 2000).

---

[4] See for example Ha et al., 2010; Tolba & Hassan, 2009; Kim & Kim, 2004, Yoo et al., 2000

2.3 Brand Dimensions in the Banking Industry

The retail banking sector is confronted with increasing competition as the level of differentiation of products and services is low (Ivanauskiene & Auruskeviciene, 2009). Developments in technology and service have evoked new approaches and ways to deal with the customer (Foo, Douglas, & Jack, 2008). There is a shift from the rather product-oriented bank to a more customer-oriented service bank (Beerli, Martín, & Quintana, 2004). This shift includes a change in marketing actions, as principles of relationship marketing become more important. In this context customer loyalty (Ivanauskiene & Auruskeviciene, 2009) and service quality (Siddiqi, 2011) are critical success factors, specifically in times of more demanding customers. The brand equity dimensions can be responsible for developing a competitive advantage which is very important in a rather homogeneous product landscape (Siddiqi, 2011). The banking industry offers a great opportunity to test Aaker's model for being applicable as brand equity measurement tool.

2.4 The Role of Brand Valuation – "Why is brand valuation such a hot topic"

Because financial people are finally starting to accept that brands are among a company's most valuable assets, and it bothers them that they can't put a specific number on the size and relative importance of that asset.

Jim Gregory - CEO of CoreBrand (2004)

Financial evaluation of brands has become a topic of considerable interest and debate[5] (Kapferer, 2008). The need for a long-term measurement of marketing activities as building of image or market share is prevalent because those activities are typically long-term oriented (Motameni & Shahrokhi,

---

[5] The debate concerning accounting issues will not be part of the thesis. For further information see Kapferer (2008, p. 504-507)

1998). The main interest comes from the M&A industry, since there is an increasing number of takeovers and bids for companies with brands (Kapferer, 2008). Ailawadi et al. (2003) list the broad purposes for measuring brand equity: (1) to guide marketing strategy and tactical decisions, (2) to assess the extendibility of a brand, (3) to track the brand's health compared with that of competitors and over time, and (4) to assign a financial value to the brand in balance sheets and financial transactions. A survey done by Sattler and PriceWaterhouse Coopers (2001) among the 100 biggest German companies concerning brand valuation yields similar outputs: first ranked purpose are brand transactions, second ranked are brand protection purposes (to estimate the compensation), third ranked is brand valuation as a tool for the strategic brand management, fourth ranked are accounting purposes and finally as a security tool for e. g. credit redemption agreement. The main issue for my thesis will be brand valuation as tool for brand management; however, I will summarize several major financial methods in the following chapters.

The next paragraph deals with the necessary standards for a valid and reliable valuation of brand equity. Ailawadi et al. (2003) list a set of "desiderata for the ideal measure" (Ailawadi, Lehmann, & Neslin, 2003, p. 2);

> 1. grounded in theory;
> 2. complete, that is, encompassing all facets of brand equity,
> yet distinct from other concepts;
> 3. diagnostic, that is, able to flag downturns or improvements
> in the brand's value and provide insights into the reasons
> for the change;
> 4. able to capture future potential in terms of future revenue
> stream and brand extendibility;
> 5. objective, so that different people computing the measure

would obtain the same value;

6. based on readily available data, so that the measure can be monitored on a regular basis for multiple brands in multiple product categories;

7. a single number, to enable easy tracking and communication;

8. intuitive and credible to senior management;

9. robust, reliable, and stable over time, yet able to reflect real changes in brand health; and

10. validated against other equity measures and constructs that are theoretically associated with brand equity

However, it is noted that no measure of brand equity will be able to fulfill all conditions. Sattler (2005) adds to the conditions above that a brand equity valuation method should be simple that also outsiders can understand the method. Further he mentions cost-benefits effects in connection with time. Specifically in the context of M&A transactions a valuation sometimes needs to be done in short time horizons. Günther and Kriegbaum (2001) further mention the necessary orientation on future events/cash flows because the brand value represents the future income potential. Additionally, the valuation must separate the product from the brand.

As one can already assume by looking at the various conditions on measuring brand equity in a reliable way, there are many problems related with the valuation. Almost every method to measure brand equity violates at least one condition (Günther & Kriegbaum, 2001). Barwise (1993) even states that "brand valuation will never be both valid and objective". He delivers three main reasons, why brand valuation is subjective: it depends on the premise of value claiming that there is no single brand value construct; brand value is not entirely separable from the rest of the company; brand valuation mostly includes forecasting of future events or cash flows which requires subjective judgments. Usually brand valuation techniques try to put a certain number, a dollar amount, on a brand. Often this is not necessary because brand valuation might contribute benefits for business performance improvements and a dollar amount is not obligatory (Wyner, 2001). Methods are mostly static and lack a "dynamic view of brand strategy" (Wyner, 2001, p. 5). In some valuation methods it is difficult to identify and quantify the value drivers of a brand (Sattler & Völckner, 2007). When determining the brand related cash flows it is difficult if not impossible to isolate only the brand related cash flows from the e. g. product related ones (Sattler & Völckner, 2007). The value of brands can change very quickly because of marketing activities such as brand extensions. It is complicated to include those changes in the valuation method.

2.5 Valuation Perspectives

2.5.1 Brand Valuation – An Overview

Combining the financial concept (equity) with a marketing-based notion has raised the "awareness of the financial value of brands" (Kapferer, 2008, p. 507). Equity indicating an ownership interest in a company refers to a long term asset built by the company (Kapferer, 2008). In fact measuring brand equity is actually measuring *brand asset*. Various approaches have been developed to measure the brand value, each tool though suitable for specific purposes (Salinas & Ambler, 2009). Goldfarb et al. (2009) define the meaning of measuring brand value. It is an exercise of two things: "(1) what the brand does for the consumer and (2) how brand equity affects a firm's competitive position, its position in the supply chain, and its decisions" (Goldfarb, Lu, & Moorthy, 2009, p. 84).

Basically there are two general motivations and directions to measure brand equity: one is the financial motivation which aims to estimate a certain value for a brand; one is the marketing motivation which aims to assess the performance of marketing activities (Keller, 1993). Going deeper into every direction, one can see a variety of approaches for different purposes to measure brand equity. The financial approaches all derive mostly from three general approaches: cost, market, income (Salinas & Ambler, 2009). Concerning the behavioral approaches there is a huge diversity within the methods.

Figure 1: Brand equity valuation - overview

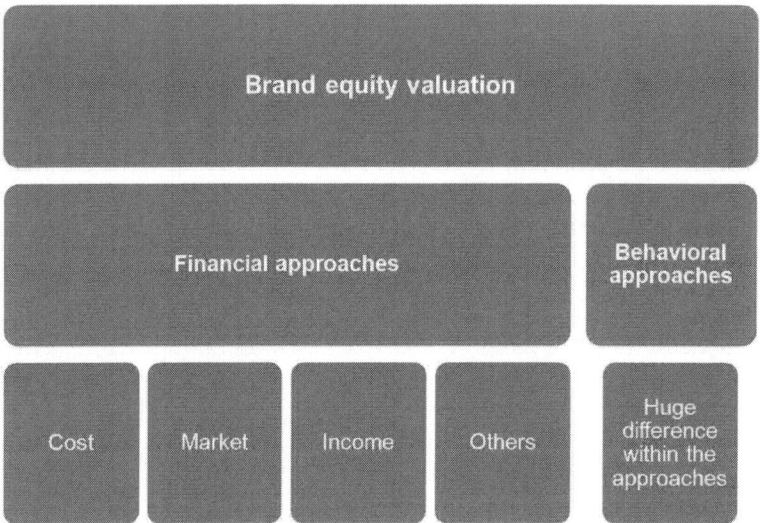

The methods summarized under "other" mainly contain valuation approaches designed by consultancies or academics that differentiate themselves from existing approaches or that use elements of more than one existing model. An overview of the approaches can be found in Salinas & Ambler (2009, p. 50).

2.5.2 Financial Perspective

A composition of financial approaches for valuing brand equity can be found in various academic works (Salinas & Ambler, 2009; Kapferer, 2008; Neal & Strauss, 2008; Sattler & Völckner, 2007; Schimanski, 2004; Esch, 2003;

Günther & Kriegbaum, 2001; Sander, 1994). Further recent articles show additional and complex new methods[6]. In this chapter the main focus lies on the more general financial approaches because most models are variations of these approaches (Salinas & Ambler, 2009). The financial perspective typically uses observational data to calculate a brand value.

Figure 2: Positioning brand valuation methods

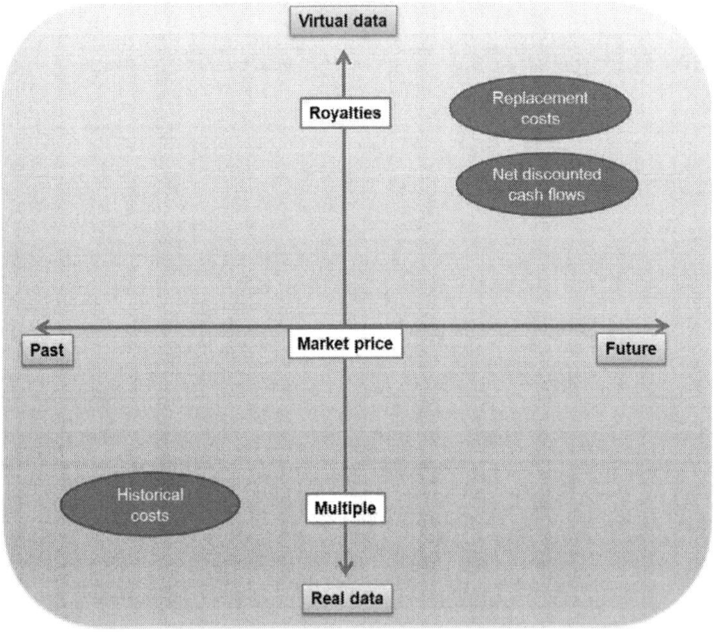

Source: Kapferer (2008), p. 513

The cost oriented model calculates the imaginary costs necessary to reestablish the brand in the same or similar way (Sattler & Völckner, 2007) or it calculates the value on the basis of all historical costs (from brand introduction until date of evaluation) (Salinas & Ambler, 2009; Sander, 1994). The historical cost approach would add "all the costs associated with a particular period: development costs, marketing costs, advertising and

---

[6] See for example (Goldfarb, Lu, & Moorthy, 2009)

communication costs, etc." (Kapferer, 2008, p. 514). This method is easy to use and logical and can provide a minimum value of the brand (Anson, 2005). Nevertheless, there are difficulties and weaknesses concerning the method (Kapferer, 2008): over what period should costs be added (some brands exist since hundreds of years)?; which costs are relevant?; what is a suitable discount rate? Even if the method delivers an output, it is a questionable value. The value would consist only of past costs concerning the input of the brand, whereas the output will not be implemented at all (Günther & Kriegbaum, 2001). It does not reflect the future potential of the brand (Anson, 2005). Additionally the approach favors "brands whose value only comes from advertising and marketing" (Kapferer, 2008, p. 514).

The other cost-oriented approach "uses current prices to estimate the cost of recreating the brand today" (Salinas & Ambler, 2009, p. 43). This method takes various characteristics into account such as awareness, absolute and relative market share, distribution network, image, leadership, quality, presence in how many countries, etc. (Kapferer, 2008). The question is how much would one have to spend and over what period to recreate such a brand? Again the model allows to estimate a minimum value for the brand (Anson, 2005) but has a couple of problems and weaknesses. It is not a good future indicator (Salinas & Ambler, 2009) and requires subjective opinions of experts (Kapferer, 2008). Again it is an input oriented model. The weakness of all cost oriented models is that "profit is not generated through investments but through market domination and leadership" (Kapferer, 2008, p. 516).

The market-based approach is sometimes possible by using open market values as reference for estimating brand equity (Salinas & Ambler, 2009). One method compares transactions of similar brands on the market (Kapferer, 2008). Simon & Sullivan (1993) propose another model. They state that the financial value of a firm comes from the "aggregate earning power"

which comes from all tangible and intangible assets. Basically all tangible assets are subtracted from the financial market value of the firm. The result is the intangible value of the firm from which the brand value can be derived. The method pays attention to the future potential of a brand because share prices reflect future cash flows in the efficient market theory (Fama, 1970). Both methods are useful when enough comparable data is available (Salinas & Ambler, 2009). Further Barth et al. (1998, p. 63) have found evidence that brand value estimates are "significantly associated with equity market values". Disadvantages of such models are the often weak data comparability (Salinas & Ambler, 2009). The model by Simon and Sullivan is only applicable to listed companies that have only one brand in their portfolio. The market for company transactions is mixed with the market for brand transactions
which increases complexity (Sander, 1994). Additionally the stock price does not reflect all marketing expenses and activities (Günther & Kriegbaum, 2001).

The income approach follows the premise "that future cash flows attributable to a brand dictate its value for its owner or a potential investor" (Salinas & Ambler, 2009, p. 42). To calculate brand equity, the value of all brand related cash flows that would not occur for an unbranded product must be predicted and discounted (Keller & Lehmann, 2006). The income models are the most common used methods as there are various models developed by specialized consultancies or academics[7]. The main methodologies are variations of the price-premium and demand drivers/brand strength analysis approach (Salinas & Ambler, 2009).

The price premium approach tries to identify the price differential of a branded product from a generic product (Trommsdorff, 2004). Basically there are two

---

[7] See Salinas & Ambler, 2009, p.45 for an overview of the different models

statistical methodologies to separate the price premium: a conjoint analysis concerning utility and product attributes and a hedonic analysis which defines the price as function of different product characteristics, brand being one of them (Sander, 1994). Advantages of this model are the easy use and the perceived removal of subjectivity in the valuation process (Salinas & Ambler, 2009). Problems that arise using that method are the lack of comparability of branded and unbranded products (Trommsdorff, 2004). Further prices can vary quickly over time due to e. g. promotion effects (Sattler, 2005). Another disadvantage is the shift of subjectivity to another level: the selection of variables or attributes for the statistical method (Salinas & Ambler, 2009).

The demand drivers/brand strength analysis determines the influence of the brand concerning the decision making process. The model looks at demand drivers *and* brand attributes and analysis them statistically or judgmentally (Salinas & Ambler, 2009). The approach tries to look at the brand as a whole, including financial and behavioral viewpoints and calculations. Yet, there is no standardized model but various approaches developed by e. g. consultancies. The advantages of the approach are the insourcing of the marketing perspective (demand drivers) and its independence from comparable data (Salinas & Ambler, 2009). Unfortunately many consultancies use the model as *black box* and outsiders cannot follow entirely the calculations (Salinas & Ambler, 2009).

Another approach of the demand driver/business strength category is the valuation by royalties. Basically it measures the license fee a company would have to pay if they would not own the brand (Salinas & Ambler, 2009). Such a method measures directly the brand's financial contribution and solves the problem of separability (Kapferer, 2008). However, the fee is not always brand specific but contains other payments due to contracts (Salinas & Ambler, 2009) and is not very common in practice (Kapferer, 2008).

2.5.3 Marketing Perspective

The behavioral perspective often uses survey data following rather qualitative methodologies in valuing a brand. Most models have different assumptions and unique methodologies, as it can be reviewed in the various behavioral approaches described in Schimanski (2004). There is a debate on whether these approaches fulfill scientific standards (Trommsdorff, 2004). Many models, however, share communalities in deriving brand equity from the brand value drivers which are characterized differently among researches (see 2.2 *Brand Dimensions*). Basically, they symbolize the sum of values each customer relates to the brand (Keller & Lehmann, 2006). Brand equity stems from the nonobjective brand values and not from product attributes (Keller & Lehmann, 2006). However, there are some aspects which are part of many theoretical and practical models (Aaker, 1996; Keller, 2003; Keller & Lehmann, 2006):

- Awareness
- Associations
- Attitude (level of attraction)
- Attachment (level of loyalty)
- Activity (purchase frequency)

The majority of approaches do not deliver a specific monetary value but certain brand characteristic numbers that can be used for brand management improvements and benchmarks.

2.6 Customer Equity vs. Brand Equity

Brand equity is related with customer equity in different ways (Keller, 2008; Leone et al., 2006). Rust et al. (2004) define customer equity as the discounted lifetime values of a firm's customer base. They relate three aspects to customer value: (1) value equity, representing the utility of a brand based on e. g. quality, price, and convenience; (2) brand equity, representing customers' perceptions beyond the objective product value; (3) relationship equity, representing customers' loyalty with a brand. They suggest a shift in being the customers more essential for a firm than the brands and products (Rust, Lemon, & Zeithaml, 2004). Lemon et al. (2001) go even further by saying that brand equity is a value driver (besides value equity and relationship equity) for customer equity. Blattberg and Deighton (1996) define customer equity as the optimal balance in what is spent on customer acquisition versus the amount spent on customer retention. As a result the central questions behind marketing activities are whether they attract new customers and whether they increase customer retention rates. The customer lifetime value concept is closely related with customer equity management. Kumer et al. (2004) have shown that customers who are selected on the basis of their customer lifetime value generate higher profits for the firm than customers selected on other customer metrics.

Although not all relations between brand equity and customer equity have been discovered (Hogan, Lemon, & Rust, 2002) both concepts share common aspects; a main driver of both concepts is customer loyalty (Leone et al., 2006). Strong customer equity helps in building a strong brand and can lead to the desired price premium. Customer equity is an essential part of customer based brand equity and can help to improve brand management. The role and importance of brand equity in the context of customer management depends on the level of customer involvement, customer experience and the perceived quality of the product before buying it (Lemon, Rust, & Zeithaml, 2001). On the other side customer equity leaves out important aspects such as better support from channel and supply chain partners, growth opportunities through brand extensions, etc. that strong brands can generate (Leone et al., 2006). In essence both concepts are inseparable connected because "there are no brands without customers, and there are no customers without brands" (Leone et al., 2006, p. 131).

Marketing activities that try to improve brand equity can also improve customer equity and vice versa (Keiningham et al., 2005).

3 Analytical Framework

Brand equity and customer equity are important aspects in the marketing decision making process, specifically both concepts are of high interest when it comes to an industry that offers rather services. In subsection 3.1 the research question will be reviewed and subsection 3.2 presents the brand equity fundament for discussing the leading hypotheses.

3.1 Research Question

The paper aims to investigate the determinants of brand equity. In order to account for the marketing-finance interface, the banking sector is chosen paying attention to both, products and services. The following hypotheses are based on the research question: *What are the determinants of brand equity in the banking industry?*

3.2 Determinants of Brand Equity

As previously noted, there are several concepts in determining the brand value drivers; yet, Aaker's model (1991, 1996) is selected to derive the leading hypotheses from. The model offers four main categories, namely brand loyalty, perceived quality, brand associations and brand awareness (the fifth category "market behavior" rather refers to market measures and is therefore not part of the subsequently presented core dimensions).

Brand loyalty

Aaker (1996) sees brand loyalty as the core dimension of brand equity to gain price premiums. Most loyalty research focuses on frequently purchased consumer goods but the concept is also important for the service industry (Rundle-Thiele & Bennet, 2001). Odin et al. (2001) state a lack of reliable measures of brand loyalty in the academic literature, however, there are two main streams defining brand loyalty according to behavioral or attitudinal terms (Mellens et al., 1996; Sun & Ghiselli, 2010). The behavioral perspective focuses on the frequency of purchases for the brand, while the attitudinal approach needs statements and attitudes of customers towards the brand (Odin et al., 2001). Attitudinal brand loyalty, being one of the brand equity components, can lead to behavioral brand loyalty (Sun & Ghiselli, 2010). The definition of brand loyalty that is most often used in research goes back to Jacoby (1971) which states that brand loyal behavior is the result of a psychological evaluation process of the brand and its alternatives. Later Olivier (1999, p. 34) also includes the behavioral and attitudinal perspective by defining brand loyalty as:

> "a deeply held commitment to rebuy or repatronize a preferred product/service consistently in the future, thereby causing repetitive same-brand or same brand-set purchasing, despite situational influences and marketing efforts having the potential to cause switching behavior".

In Aaker's view (1991) loyalty refers to the probability a customer will switch to another brand, especially if there are changes in prices or other features. All definitions and concepts share the common aspect of generating repurchases and/or being able to demand price premiums which ultimately creates value. Therefore the following hypothesis is formulated:

H1.   Brand loyalty has a positive and significant impact on brand equity.
Perceived quality/service
Perceived quality (service) is defined as the consumer's overall judgment about a product's excellence or superiority with respect to its original purpose (Zeithaml, 1988). In service industries like the banking sector, not only the quality of products is important, but also to a similar extent services around

those rather intangible products. Subsequently perceived quality and service are treated as one construct with two dimensions. Sethuraman and Cole (1997) show that perceived quality can explain considerable amounts of variance in price premium, consumers are willing to pay. Aaker (1996) calls perceived quality a key dimension for brand equity, as it is associated with price premiums, price elasticities, brand usage and even stock returns. High perceived quality will lead the consumer to buy one product instead of other competing ones, therefore high perceived quality should increase brand equity (Yoo, Donthu, & Lee, 2000). Based on these points the following hypothesis is formulated:

H2. *Perceived quality and service has a positive and significant impact on brand equity.*

Brand awareness
According to Keller (2008) brand awareness consists of *brand recognition* and *brand recall*. Brand recognition is the "consumers' ability to confirm prior exposure to the brand when given the brand as a cue" (Keller, 2008, p. 54). Brand recall describes the consumers' ability to recall a specific brand from memory when given the product category (Keller, 2008). If a customer recognizes and recalls a brand, the customer is more likely to buy this familiar brand (Sun & Ghiselli, 2010). Aaker (1996) states that awareness can even drive perceptions and attitudes towards a brand. Familiarity with a brand is needed to set a certain image in the minds of consumers and is further an important value driver of brand equity (Esch, 2003). Positive brand awareness can lead to learning, consideration and choice advantages[8] which all support the decision making process (Keller, 2008). Hence the next hypothesis follows:

---

[8] See Keller (2008, pp. 54-55) for further details

H3.   Brand awareness has a positive and significant impact on brand equity

Brand associations

Brand associations are defined as "anything linked in memory to a brand" (Aaker, 1991, p. 109). They are directly connected with brand image which consists of different associations "organized in some meaningful way" (Aaker, 1991, p. 109). Keller (1993) states that brand image is carried via associations with the brand that are formed about attributes and personal benefits of the brand. Favorable associations are crucial during the buying decision and firms try to enhance those associations by building a certain brand image. Aaker (1991) has listed the advantages of positive brand associations: they help to differentiate the brand, process information, generate a reason to buy a brand, create a positive attitude towards the brand and provide the basis for further extensions. In essence positive brand associations are a key element in the buying decision and hence can increase brand equity. As a result the fourth hypothesis is:

H4.   Brand associations have a positive and significant impact on brand equity.

Inter-item correlations

While it seems obvious that the brand equity dimensions also influence each other, the inter-correlations in the banking sector remain unclear. In general Aaker (1991) indicates a direct relation between brand loyalty and perceived quality. Beerli et al. (2004) have found a direct relationship between customer satisfaction and perceived service quality which both ultimately influence brand loyalty. Past research has shown the importance of brand loyalty to brand equity (Atilgan, Aksoy, & Akinci, 2005). Sirgy et al. (2008) discovered the moderating role of brand awareness affecting customer loyalty. Esch (2003) hints that awareness is a very important brand value driver and essential in building brand image and loyalty. Based on these findings the following hypotheses were proposed:

H5.

    a) Perceived service quality has a positive and significant impact on brand loyalty.

    b) Customer satisfaction has a positive and significant impact on brand loyalty.

    c) Brand awareness has a positive and significant impact on brand loyalty.

    d) Brand associations have a positive and significant impact on brand loyalty.

Aaker (1991, 1996) further points out that perceived quality can be influenced by all other brand equity constructs. As a result perceived quality can be created without having the consumer experiencing the brand but with e. g. the brand's logo, other images, word of mouth, etc. Beerli et al. (2004) have found customer satisfaction to be an antecedent of perceived service quality. Since in most banks the service quality plays a major role, I relate those brand equity items to perceived service quality. To account for these relations, the following hypotheses were formed:

H6.

    a) Customer satisfaction has a positive and significant impact on perceived service quality.

    b) Brand awareness has a positive and significant impact on perceived service quality.

    c) Brand associations have a positive and significant impact on perceived service quality.

    d) Brand loyalty has a positive and significant impact on perceived service quality.

Figure 3: Conceptual model

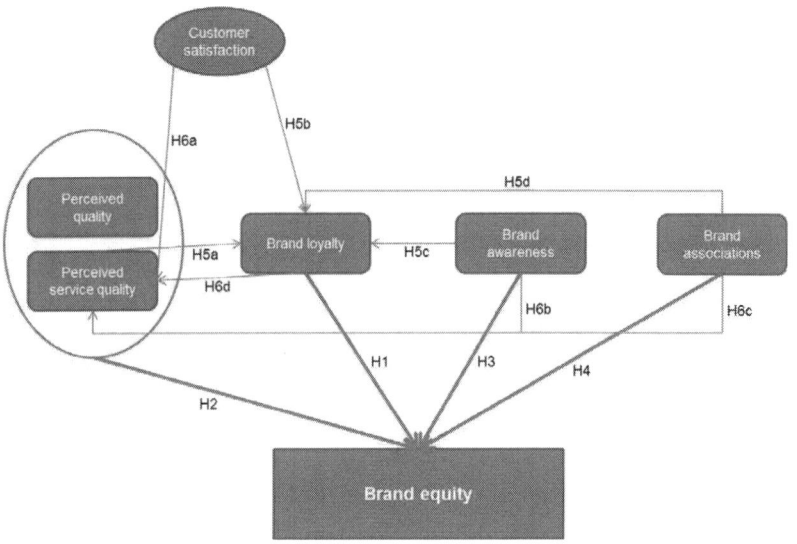

4 Methodology

A questionnaire framework has been designed in order to test the above hypotheses. The main participation comes from the internet, since the questionnaire was put online[9], however, some print-out versions have been distributed as well. The target market are banking clients, hence the questionnaire is developed for a cross sectional selected population from Germany and the Netherlands. Three dummy variables are used for classification reasons: gender, age and educational background. For products there are several already validated measurement items of the dimensions of brand equity, yet, for services little research has been conducted (Sun & Ghiselli, 2010). In the banking industry products and services are treated both important for clients, however, items are mainly taken from measurements of brand equity for products: in total 26 items are selected to test the hypotheses. Three items each are taken from Beerli et al. (2004, p. 262) to

---

[9] I used the free questionnaire design at www.thesistools.com

measure brand loyalty and customer satisfaction. Both items were tested for the retail banking sector and have been used in recent academic research (Afsar et al., 2010), thus represent a good fit for the model. For perceived quality six items are selected from Yoo et al. (2000, p. 203). Perceived service consists of four items taken from Cronin & Brady (2001, p. 46). The scales are originally designed for the banking industry; hence represent a good fit for the model. To account for brand awareness, three items are used from Yoo et al. (2000, p. 203). For brand associations three items stem from Yoo et al. (2000, p. 203). Finally, for overall brand equity, four items are taken from Yoo et al. (2000, p. 203). On the basis of these items, a questionnaire has been developed to check the aspects of brand equity and its dimensions. Most measures are selected from Yoo et al. (2000) because their empirical study tested Aaker's (1991, 1996) brand equity model. Their scale development model is universally accepted by academics and practioners (Atilgan, Aksoy, & Akinci, 2005).

The survey asks participants to rate products/services of their house bank on the basis of the four brand equity dimensions and overall brand equity on a seven-point scale. Interval data allows to apply various statistical techniques. In order to test the main hypotheses a regression model is applied, analysing the degree of variation the independent variables are able to explain (Malhotra, 2007). Correlations show the coherence of the different items.

Table 2: Brand equity dimensions

Brand loyalty		Alpha[10]: 0.7829
	I do not like to change to another bank	
LO1	because I value the selected bank.	
LO2	I am a customer loyal to my bank.	
	I would always recommend my bank to	
LO3	someone who seeks my advice.	

---

[10] Scale measured by the authors who originally used the questions

Customer satisfaction   0.8106

CS1   To what extent does this bank live up to your general expectations of it?

CS2   Imagine the perfect bank. How far and/or close does this bank come to your ideal?

CS3   Given your experience with this bank, how satisfied or dissatisfied are you with it overall?

Perceived quality

PQ1	X is of high quality.	0.87
PQ2	The likely quality of X is extremely high.	0.93
PQ3	The likelihood that X would be functional is very high.	0.82
PQ4	The likelihood that X is reliable is very high.	0.87
PQ5	X must be of very good quality.	0.84
PQ6	X appears to be of very poor quality.	0.60

Service quality   0.87-0.93

SQ1   I would say that XYZ's physical environment is one of the best in its industry.

SQ2   I would rate XYZ's physical environment highly.

SQ3   I would say that XYZ provides superior service.

SQ4   I believe XYZ offers excellent service.

Brand awareness

AW1	I know what X looks like.	0.92
AW2	I can recognize X among other competing brands.	0.92
AW3	I am aware of X.	0.90

Brand associations

AS1	Some characteristics of X come to my mind quickly.	0.79
AS2	I can quickly recall the symbol or logo of X.	0.85
AS3	I have difficulty in imagining X in my mind.	0.66

Brand equity

BE1	It makes sense to buy X instead of any other brand, even if they are the same.	0.79
BE2	Even if another brand has same features as X, I would prefer to buy X.	0.94
BE3	If there is another brand as good as X, I prefer to buy X.	0.94
BE4	If another brand is not different from X in any way, it seems smarter to purchase X.	0.85

5 Results

5.1 Pre-analysis and Assumptions

After being online for one month I received in total 105 filled participations. Most people participated over the internet and I received additional nine filled paper versions. One case had to be excluded from analysis because the participant had given the same answers for every question, even for the reversely framed ones. In total 104 cases were used for analysis. 75% of the participants were male, 85% aged below 30 and 94% already obtained a university degree (most of the participants were students). The two negatively framed items PQ6 and AS3 have been reversely coded to be suitable for analysis.

The data has been checked for validity and reliability. Validity of the items is approved, since all items were taken from already existing and statistically proven journal articles. In order to test the suitability for using the items in the context of the banking questionnaire design, Cronbach's alpha scores were evaluated. Every statement yields a Cronbach's alpha above 0.913 (see appendix table 17) indicating a reliable scale. The overall scale for each brand equity dimension used in this study is shown in table 3:

Table 3: Reliability of the items

Brand equity dimension	Alpha
Brand loyalty	0.860
Perceived quality and service	0.915
Brand awareness	0.925
Brand associations	0.699
Brand equity	0.844
Customer satisfaction	*0.864*

All dimensions have an alpha above the critical level of 0.7 (except for brand associations which scores 0.699). Overall reliability is approved. To obtain a first overview of the results, the means of the items were calculated in table 4:

Table 4: Descriptives of the four main brand equity dimensions

Descriptive Statistics

	N	Minimum	Maximum	Mean	Std. Deviation
LO1	104	2	7	5,26	1,088
LO2	104	2	7	5,31	1,175
LO3	104	2	7	5,38	1,090
PQ1	104	2	7	5,44	,912
PQ2	103	2	7	5,34	,996
PQ3	103	2	7	5,51	,979
PQ4	103	2	7	5,82	,813
PQ5	104	2	7	5,61	,841
PQ6_reversed	104	2	7	5,88	,992
SQ1	103	1	7	4,52	1,119
SQ2	103	1	7	4,69	1,076
SQ3	104	2	7	5,11	,913
SQ4	104	1	7	4,81	1,080
AW1	104	1	7	6,11	,913
AW2	104	1	7	5,89	1,230
AW3	104	1	7	6,07	1,007
AS1	104	2	7	5,66	1,058
AS2	104	1	7	5,98	1,097
AS3_reversed	104	1	7	5,91	1,422

A first conclusion from the means is that on average respondents seem to be satisfied with their banks and the services and are aware of certain brand characteristics.

The next step in the analysis includes the evaluation of the causal relationships among the main brand equity dimensions. Therefore a correlations of the four main dimensions has been conducted:

Table 5: Correlations of the four main brand equity dimensions

Correlations					
		Brand_loyalty	Perceived_qu ality_and_ser vice	Brand_aware ness	Brand_assoc iations
Brand_loyalty	Pearson Correlation	1			
Perceived_qu ality_and_ser	Pearson Correlation	,749**	1		
Brand_aware ness	Pearson Correlation	.086	.106	1	
Brand_assoc iations	Pearson Correlation	,205*	.114	,793**	1

** Correlation is significant at the 0.01 level (two-tailed)

* Correlation is significant at the 0.05 level (two-tailed)

After evaluating the inter-item correlations and the dimension correlations there is a high and significant correlation between *brand_loyalty* and *perceived_quality_and_service*. Specifically *LO1* and *LO3* highly correlate with *PQ1, PQ2, PQ3* and *SQ3* (correlation with other quality and service items is at a rather medium but significant level). *Brand_awareness* and *brand_associations* highly and significantly correlate. Particularly *AS2* correlates with *AW1, AW2* and *AW3* at a level above 0.8. To conclude from the correlation matrix it can be recognized that in general *brand_loyalty* and *perceived_quality_and_service* correlate strongly as well as *brand_awareness* and *brand_associations*.

Before initializing regression analysis, the data needs to be checked for the core regression assumptions including normality, linearity homoscedasticity and outliers might be considered to be removed. The normal probability plot (see appendix figure 6) as well as the histogram (see appendix figure 5) imply no major deviations from normality. Linearity is additionally supported. To account for homoscedasticity a scatterplot of the standardized residuals is evaluated (see figure 4 below). Most of the cases are concentrated around the center of the plot further indicating no systematic pattern implying no violation of the assumption. The scatterplot can also detect possible outliers which should be outside the +3.3/-3.3 borders (Tabachnik & Fidell, 2007). Two cases are outside the boundaries and are therefore deleted for the regression analysis (see figure 4).

Figure 4: Scatterplot

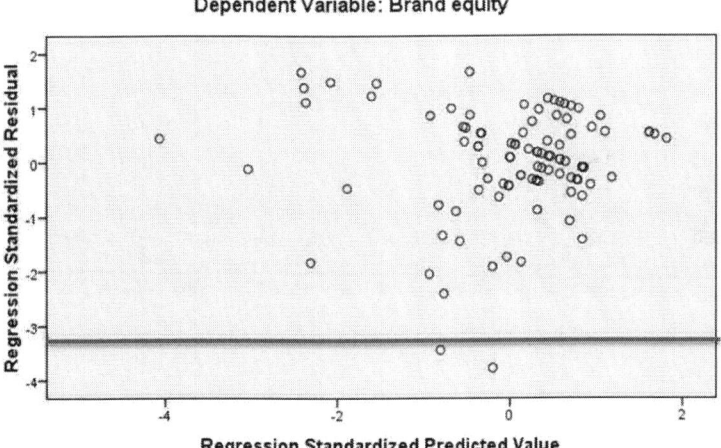

Multicollinearity is deliberately not tested for, since the independent variables represent the four main brand equity dimensions proposed by Aaker (1991) and are predefined for analysis. A total of 102 cases remain for further analysis.

5.2 Regression Analysis – Test of the Main Hypotheses

Table 6: Model summary

Model Summary[b]

Model	R	R Square	Adjusted R Square	Std. Error of the Estimate
1	,555[a]	,308	,279	,810

a. Predictors: (Constant), Brand_associations, Perceived_quality_and_service, Brand_loyalty, Brand_awareness

b. Dependent Variable: Brand_equity

Table 7: Anova

ANOVA[b]

Model		Sum of Squares	df	Mean Square	F	Sig.
1	Regression	27,501	4	6,875	10,480	,000[a]
	Residual	61,667	94	,656		
	Total	89,167	98			

a. Predictors: (Constant), Brand_associations, Perceived_quality_and_service, Brand_loyalty, Brand_awareness

b. Dependent Variable: Brand_equity

The proposed model is able to explain 30.8% of the variance in *brand_equity* which can be interpreted as a good result since the model consists of only four variables. The model reaches statistical significance (see table 7).

Table 8: Main results

Coefficients[a]

Model		Unstandardized Coefficients		Standardized Coefficients			Correlations		
		B	Std. Error	Beta	t	Sig.	order	Partial	Part
1	(Constant)	.308	.757		.407	.685			
	Brand_loyalty	.248	.130	.258	1.904	.060	.489	.193	.163
	Perceived_quality_and_service	.336	.173	.256	1.938	.056	.476	.196	.166
	Brand_awareness	.078	.139	.081	.562	.575	.247	.058	.048
	Brand_associations	.140	.146	.140	.956	.342	.290	.098	.082

Table 8 shows the contribution of the four independent variables in explaining the variance in *brand_equity*. While two variables (*brand_awareness* and *brand_associations*) are non-significant with low beta coefficients, *brand_loyalty* and *perceived_quality_and_service* show significance at the 10% level. The latter two variables both have strong positive beta coefficients indicating a high contribution to explaining brand equity. Squaring the part correlations shows the unique contribution of the variable to the overall R^2 which is nearly equal for both variables (around 2.7%). Coming back to the hypotheses, the model shows support for H1. *Brand_loyalty* has a positive standardized beta (0.258) coefficient indicating a positive impact on brand equity and being significant at the 10% level (almost at the 5% level). H2 is also supported by the model, since *perceived_quality_and_service* shows a positive standardized beta coefficient (0.256) being significant at the 10% level (almost at the 5% level). H3 is not supported: The standardized beta value of *brand_awareness* is very low and highly insignificant. *Brand_associations* also shows insignificant coefficients. Therefore H4 is not supported for the same reasons.

5.3 Regression Analysis – Test of the Remaining Hypotheses

In order to test H5 a regression has been conducted. The dependent variable is *brand_loyalty*; the independent variables are *perceived_service*, *customer_satisfaction*, *brand_awareness* and *brand_associations*. Not surprisingly, from a logical point of view, *customer_satisfaction* highly correlates with *brand_loyalty* and *perceived_service* (see table 9).

Table 9: Correlations II

		Correlations				
		Brand_loyalty	Perceived_service	Customer_satisfaction	Brand_awareness	Brand_associations
Pearson Correlation	Brand_loyalty	1.000				
	Perceived_service	.528	1.000			
	Customer_satisfaction	.800	.659	1.000		
	Brand_awareness	.101	.170	.070	1.000	
	Brand_associations	.215	.140	.130	.792	1.000
Sig. (1-tailed)	Brand_loyalty	.				
	Perceived_service	.000	.			
	Customer_satisfaction	.000	.000	.		
	Brand_awareness	.156	.045	.242	.	
	Brand_associations	.015	.081	.096	.000	.

The regression analysis shows the following output:

Table 10: Model summary II

Model Summary[b]

Model	R	R Square	Adjusted R Square	Std. Error of the Estimate
1	,811[a]	,657	,643	,592

a. Predictors: (Constant), Brand_associations,
Customer_satisfaction, Perceived_service, Brand_awareness

b. Dependent Variable: Brand_loyalty

Table 11: Anova II

ANOVA[b]

Model		Sum of Squares	df	Mean Square	F	Sig.
1	Regression	64,570	4	16,142	46,027	,000[a]
	Residual	33,669	96	,351		
	Total	98,239	100			

a. Predictors: (Constant), Brand_associations, Customer_satisfaction, Perceived_service, Brand_awareness

b. Dependent Variable: Brand_loyalty

Table 12: Main results II

Coefficients[a]

Model		Unstandardized Coefficients		Standardized Coefficients	t	Sig.	Correlations		
		B	Std. Error	Beta			order	Partial	Part
1	(Constant)	.330	.502		.656	.513			
	Perceived_service	.011	.096	.009	.114	.909	.528	.012	.007
	Customer_satisfaction	.870	.090	.775	9.629	.000	.800	.701	.575
	Brand_awareness	-.119	.100	-.119	-1.194	.235	.101	-.121	-.071
	Brand_associations	.214	.103	.207	2.092	.039	.215	.209	.125

The model is able to explain 65.7% of the variance in *brand_loyalty* and reaches statistical significance. The highest contribution to the model delivers *customer_satisfaction* with a standardized beta of 0.775 while being significant at the 5% level. The unique contribution of the variable to the overall R^2 is remarkably high with 33%. *Brand_associations* also have a positive standardized beta of 0.207 (significant at the 5% level), but has a rather low contribution to R^2 (1.6%). The remaining two variables *perceived_service* and *brand_awareness* both have low standardized betas and are not significant. Therefore hypotheses H5 b) and d) are supported, while H5 a) and c) are not supported and must be rejected.

To test H6 (Aaker's (1991, 1996) suggested influence of the brand equity dimensions on perceived service quality) a regression analysis has been conducted. The dependent variable is *perceived_service*; the independent variables are *brand_loyalty*, *customer_satisfaction*, *brand_awareness* and *brand_associations*.

Table 13: Model summary III

Model Summary[b]

Model	R	R Square	Adjusted R Square	Std. Error of the Estimate
1	,674[a]	,454	,431	,627

a. Predictors: (Constant), Brand_loyalty, Brand_awareness, Customer_satisfaction, Brand_associations

b. Dependent Variable: Perceived_service

Table 14: Anova III

ANOVA[b]

Model		Sum of Squares	df	Mean Square	F	Sig.
1	Regression	31,363	4	7,841	19,973	,000[a]
	Residual	37,686	96	,393		
	Total	69,050	100			

a. Predictors: (Constant), Brand_loyalty, Brand_awareness, Customer_satisfaction, Brand_associations

b. Dependent Variable: Perceived_service

Table 15: Main results III

Coefficients[a]

Model		Unstandardized Coefficients		Standardized Coefficients	t	Sig.	Correlations		
		B	Std. Error	Beta			order	Partial	Part
1	(Constant)	1.150	.520		2.213	.029			
	Customer_satisfaction	.609	.119	.647	5.129	.000	.659	.464	.387
	Brand_awareness	.183	.105	.218	1.753	.083	.170	.176	.132
	Brand_associations	-.104	.110	-.120	-.945	.347	.140	-.096	-.071
	Brand_loyalty	.012	.108	.015	.114	.909	.528	.012	.009

The model is able to explain 45.4% of the variance in *perceived_service* (significant). The highest contribution generates *customer_satisfaction* with a standardized beta of 0.647 while being significant at the 5% level. Again the variable contributes highly to the overall R^2 with 15%. *Brand_awareness* has a positive standardized beta of 0.218 but is only significant at the 10% level and has a low unique contribution to R^2 (1.7%). *Brand_associations* and *brand_loyalty* show no significant results. Therefore H6 a) receives strong support. H6 b) receives weak support (significance at 10% level). H6 c) and d) are not supported by the model and must be rejected.

Table 16: Summary results

Hypothesis		Supported/not supported
H1	--------------→	Supported
H2	--------------→	Supported
H3	--------------→	Not supported
H4	--------------→	Not supported
H5a	--------------→	Not supported
H5b	--------------→	Supported
H5c	--------------→	Not supported
H5d	--------------→	Supported
H6a	--------------→	Supported
H6b	--------------→	Supported
H6c	--------------→	Not supported
H6d	--------------→	Not supported

6 Discussion

The discussion is centered around the possible consequences and shortcomings of the presented results in this study. The section additionally seeks a connection between the specific bank related results and the more general brand equity literature presented in section 2, *Literature Review*. An aspect of much interest is whether the results support or contradict current viewpoints of the traditionally more product related brand equity concepts. I follow the idea of Bem (1987, p. 187) who designs the discussion section in a way that it symbolizes "the bottom of the hourglass-shaped format and thus proceeds from specific matters [...] to more general concerns". Further the author suggests to stick to the essential themes and to focus on positive advancements. Relying on Bem's (1987) advice, I start the discussion with the topic *brand equity in the banking context*, expanding it to a broader perspective and finally connecting it to the general brand equity literature. First, I comment on the pure results which were derived from a questionnaire following the general brand equity dimensions proposed by Aaker (1991, 1996) and relate the results to other academic findings in this context. Second, the results are put into a broader perspective to show their consequences and shortcomings for the existing brand equity literature. The second part builds a bridge of the specific findings of this study to the rather general oriented literature review. This study tries to empirically test Aakers' brand equity dimensions and their applicability in the context of brand value in the banking sector. The results show support for some of Aakers' suggestions that brand loyalty and perceived quality positively influence brand equity (H1 and H2), yet the value creating character of the dimensions brand awareness and brand associations is not supported by the study (H3 and H4).

Brand loyalty, perceived quality and customer satisfaction as one depending influential construct

The findings concerning the first hypothesis H1 support the general opinion of brand loyalty in the academic literature which announces brand loyalty as one of the core dimensions of brand equity being responsible for the continuous (re-)purchase of goods and services. Especially in an industry which is heavily built on values such as trust and reliability, it seems to be a logical conclusion that loyalty is a very important value driver. Loyalty is very closely connected to customer satisfaction, as the findings in this study reveal a strong correlation of 0.8. This aspect seems particularly important when relating customer satisfaction to the concept of *word-of-mouth* (Richins, 1983). Diener and Greyser (1978) already found over 30 years ago that 34% of the dissatisfied customers speak to others about their dissatisfaction. Taking the internet and social networking of today into account, one can easily assume that the news of dissatisfied customers will spread more quickly in a global way. As a concluding remark, one can say that brand loyalty remains a very important topic for banks, as they cannot risk losing customers because of the potential bad *word-of-mouth* effects.

However, brand loyalty and customer satisfaction are also significantly related to perceived service quality, as high correlations reveal (brand loyalty correlates 0.749 with perceived quality and service; customer satisfaction correlates 0.659 with perceived service). In the academic literature perceived quality is seen as a construct that can explain considerable price variations (Sethuraman & Cole, 1997) and Aaker (1996) defines it as another core dimension of brand equity. Especially in an industry with a rather homogeneous product landscape, service quality is a necessary feature that creates value. It further helps to differentiate the brand from others because most of the products in the banking industry are available at every bank (Barnes & Howlett, 1998). The statistical support for H2 continues this reasoning. Due to the high correlations of customer satisfaction, brand loyalty and perceived service quality, this study recommends not to disregard either of the dimensions. All three can be seen as one depending construct that is a very important value driver for brand equity in the banking industry.

The dependence of brand loyalty and perceived quality is regarded differently in the academic literature: According to Beerli et al. (2004) loyalty and perceived quality are the result of customer satisfaction which has to be implemented first. Satisfied customers rate the bank's quality at a high level in order to avoid personal dissonance (Beerli, Martín, & Quintana, 2004). This finding and the results of my study stand in contrast to what Parasuraman et al. (1985) and Cronin and Taylor (1992) found. Their research supports the view that "perceived service quality in fact leads to satisfaction" (Cronin & Taylor, 1992, p. 64), so quality must be present first. Aaker (1996) sees customer satisfaction closely connected to brand loyalty, but calls loyalty the main influential driver behind the construct. Nonetheless, all academics share the opinion that loyalty, perceived quality and customer satisfaction have a positive influence on brand equity which is also supported by my study.

The influence of brand awareness and brand associations

My findings do not support the academic opinion that brand awareness is one influential dimension of brand equity. Specifically Keller (2008) constituted several advantages, brand awareness possibly contributes to creating brand equity. The results of this study show almost no explanatory power and are insignificant. Nonetheless, this insignificance is in line with other academic findings that used Aaker's model to explain brand equity. Atilgan et al. (2005) who applied the model in the context of the beverage industry also attributed low explanatory power to brand awareness. Tong and Hawley (2009) come to similar results concerning the influence of brand awareness. Both studies are related to tangible products; beverage industry in turkey and sportswear market in china. Bailey and Ball (2006) who investigated the meanings of brand equity in the hotel industry state that brand names themselves do not contribute to success. Apparently just being aware of a brand does not increase brand equity, at least in the banking industry. The majority of participants were aware of their bank and competing brands, yet quality, satisfaction and loyalty play a more important role in creating brand value. Brand awareness is highly related to brand associations in this study, as a correlation of 0.792 implies. Therefore, the findings concerning the influential behavior of brand associations on brand equity are not surprising: H4 does not receive support contradicting Keller (1993) and Aaker (1991) who name brand associations an important aspect in purchase decisions. This study attributes almost no explanatory power to brand associations in explaining brand equity. Once again these findings suggest that brand names as well as mental associations do not seem to play an important role for customers in evaluating their bank. Other academic papers come to divergent results. Atilgan et al. (2005) come to similar results as my study. The authors find weak influence of brand associations on brand equity. On the other hand Tong and Hawley (2009) claim brand associations to have a positive and significant effect on brand equity. Their study reveals brand associations to be one of the most influencing dimensions for brand equity.

Causal relationships of brand equity dimensions and brand loyalty

To account for the inter-item causal relationships, H5 tests the impact of brand equity dimensions on brand loyalty. From a logical point of view, loyalty only can develop from an ongoing customer relationship. Surprisingly the results of this study show no statistical significant impact of perceived service quality on brand loyalty. Customer satisfaction positively influences brand loyalty which is generally supported in other academic papers, e. g. Beerli et al. (2004). The authors show a positive influence of customer satisfaction on perceived service quality; vice versa low influence is shown. Satisfaction is claimed to be an antecedent of perceived service quality (Beerli et al., 2004), however, Kumar et al. (2010) also discover a positive influence of service quality on satisfaction. These findings are also supported by the results of this study, since customer satisfaction and perceived service quality correlate at a high and significant level (0.659), but only customer satisfaction has explanatory power to explain brand loyalty. Again brand awareness has no positive and significant effect on brand loyalty. This finding stands in contrast to what Sirgy et al. (2008) found: their results indicate positive effects of sponsorships on brand loyalty under the condition that the customers are aware of the brand. Awareness is a premise to get loyalty. Nonetheless, brand associations have a little positive and significant effect on brand loyalty, implying that customers build a sort of personal relationship with their bank in which they associate certain things with the bank/brand. However, the influence on loyalty is at a rather low level.

Causal relationships of brand equity dimensions and perceived service quality
H6 tests the influence of the brand equity dimensions on perceived service quality, as Aaker (1991) suggests an inter-dependence. Customer satisfaction has a positive and significant impact on perceived service quality which is in line with the findings of Beerli et al. (2004). Brand awareness has also an effect on perceived service quality, although at a rather low level and only significant at the 10% level. However, Aaker's suggestion seems to be right that perceived quality can be created without the customer even experiencing the brand, but by e. g. the logo or *word-of-mouth*. Brand loyalty and brand associations have no significant effect on perceived service quality which is in line with previous findings. Loyalty develops a long with customer satisfaction and perceived service quality and does not create them by itself.

Expanding the perspective
The academic branding literature distinguishes between tangible (product) industries and intangible (service) industries but most branding literature is biased towards products (Turley & Moore, 1995). Specifically brand equity literature is far greater concerned with products than with intangibles (Mackay, 2001). Krishnan and Hartline (2001, p. 328) even suggest a lack of "basic understanding" for brand equity in the service industry. However, brand equity remains important for service industries, either in the context of brand strategies or valuation purposes for e. g. mergers. Mackay (2001, p. 211)

suggests that "the way that branding is applied and the way its effectiveness is measured may differ between products and services", although not knowing how they might differ. His study shows that several brand equity dimensions (awareness and familiarity aspects) can be used in either context; brand equity measurements for products and for services. This study contributes to an understanding of brand equity in a service dominant sector. Widely accepted and used brand equity dimensions that rather relate to tangible products are applied in the service industry. While studies using a similar methodology in the tangible product industry (Tong and Hawley, 2009 - sportswear; Atilgan et al., 2005 – beverages) show brand loyalty and brand associations to be influential factors of brand equity, this study reveals brand loyalty and perceived quality and service to have a positive influence. Brand loyalty seems to be very important either for product or service industries. In product industries the associations with the brand are important for the repurchase behavior; in this study, perceived quality in connection with customer satisfaction is one of the main value drivers. As a result this study supports the idea of Mackay (2001) that branding is different in a way, depending on the industry. However, this study also supports communalities between the industries (brand loyalty). Krishnan and Hartline (2001, p. 336) find support for more communalities between both industries by stating "that tangible goods and search-dominant services are very similar in terms of brand equity indices and the importance of brand equity".

A topic of much interest is the definition of brand equity dimensions or value drivers. While this study uses the widely accepted model of Aaker (1991, 1996), there are several other propositions for brand equity dimensions (see *2.2 Brand Dimensions*). An often referred brand equity dimension is brand image in connection with brand awareness (Esch, 2003; Sattler, 2005; Keller 2008). Aaker implements brand image in his dimension brand associations. A survey among practitioners has revealed brand image to be the most important brand value driver (Sattler & Völckner, 2007). On the other hand this study does not support the idea of brand image/associations being one of the most important factors in explaining brand equity. A possible explanation might be that brand image is especially important when it comes to tangible products the customer can experience, touch and feel. This study suggests that brand associations are not an important aspect in the banking sector in explaining brand equity. In service dominant industries, where no tangible products exist, brand image/associations seem to weigh less than in other industries. Kayaman and Arasli (2007) found that brand awareness does not play an influential role in determining brand equity for the hotel industry. Again loyalty and quality are the main value drivers. Berry (2000) points out the importance of the company as a whole unit when dealing with product intangibility in service industries ("the company becomes the brand"). A crucial step for creating a strong brand is to be different from other service providers (Berry, 2000).

Finally the results of this study can improve brand valuation according to the demand driver input. More specifically brands can be measured according to certain demand drivers; Salinas and Ambler (2009, p. 46) define those measurements as "Demand Drivers/Brand Strength Analysis". The tool tries to "determine the influence of the brand in the decision making process. It is based on the analysis of demand drivers and / or brand attributes" (Salinas & Ambler, 2009, p. 46). The findings help to determine the value drivers for brand equity in the banking sector according to their importance. The validity of the results might be expanded to other valuation approaches to e. g. other service industries. The explanatory power of the standardized input variables is updated. The results suggest brand loyalty in connection with perceived quality and customer satisfaction to be the most important demand drivers in evaluating the brand. On the other hand brand awareness and brand associations seem to loom less in the banking sector.

7 Summary

7.1 Theoretical Implications

With respect to the presented interpretations in section *6 Discussion,* this chapter finalizes and expands the broader picture, brand equity and brand valuation represents in the academic literature. According to Huff (1999, p. 92) the closing chapter should pull the reader "back to the big picture with a conclusion so they will remember the broadest possible application". Section *2 Literature Review* exposes brand equity as a complex construct which cannot be grasped easily. While either academics or practitioners agree on the huge value potential, brand equity generates within a company, neither a definition nor a generally accepted measurement approach exists (Trommsdorff, 2004). Most definitions are built around certain brand dimensions which differ across definitions. Ferjani et al. (2009, p. 861) state that "brand equity for a given brand vary considerably across methods". The bottom line of these results is that brand dimensions and brand values seem to differ from industry to industry or even from company to company. Sander (1994) criticizes brand valuation methods as they do not properly incorporate a brand's individuality. This individuality suggests that brand equity must be assessed separately for different industry sectors.

This study uses Aaker's (1991, 1996) proposed brand equity dimensions to test their explanatory power to measure brand equity in the banking sector. The test of the effects of brand equity dimensions on brand equity is announced by Yoo et al. (2000, p. 207) as "a very important future research issue". My results imply a lower importance and significance of brand awareness and associations in evaluating brand equity in the banking sector. The results might hold for other service dominant industries, since most of the existing brand equity literature refers to product dominant industries (Mackay, 2001). This study contributes to a better understanding of the important value drivers of brand equity in a service dominant industry. Keller and Lehmann

(2006) provide three basic brand performance measurement approaches: customer based, company based and financial based. The findings can improve customer based evaluation models, since the important values from a customers' point of view are shown. Nonetheless, the individuality of a brand must not be disregarded, since various academic brand equity studies deliver divergent brand equity dimensions depending on the industry they were conducted. As a result, consequences for possible brand positionings or other marketing actions must be drawn according to the relevant brand equity literature; however, similarities across industries can be identified.

7.2 Managerial Implications

The managerial implications of this study are also of high relevance, specifically in the field of brand management and advertisement. The findings show that brand equity is best explained by the three variables brand loyalty, perceived quality and customer satisfaction. Brand names or associations on the other hand show no statistical relevance. Brand managers can use the model of this study as a strategic tool to evaluate marketing options. Companies may learn to improve their understanding of the customer value by looking at the relevant customer metrics. It provides information about differentiation possibilities from other brands and can help the strategic decision making process in terms of branding or advertisement issues. The tool can assist in developing new advertising campaigns, as managers can clearly identify the most relevant and important customer metrics that increase brand equity.

In addition my findings can help to improve the role of marketing in a financial institution. Rust et al. (2004) state that marketing must show its value creating character, by demonstrating how behavioral measures drive financial measures. Since brand equity is one of the most valuable assets within a company, my model can show the contribution to this value, thereby strengthening the role of marketing. Srinivasan and Hanssens (2009) claim that marketing is often underestimated because market based assets such as brand equity or customer value are invisible/intangible and hard to measure. My findings contribute to a better understanding of market based assets and their impact. Marketing managers can use the findings to verify certain marketing actions and their value creating character.

7.3 Limitations

I build the limitations section on two major aspects. One contains possible limitations resulting from the analytical framework and one refers to possible biases and shortcomings in the questionnaire design. Starting with the analytical model this study has some limitations: the model refers only to Aakers' brand equity dimensions; however, there are several other possible ways to determine brand equity[11]. Aakers' dimensions rather relate to product industries, whereas there may be other possibilities, specifically for the service sector. The overall model considers only qualitative inputs from the questionnaire and does not incorporate financial values. As a result the model cannot calculate any monetary brand value. The participants of the questionnaire were mainly students; 85% aged below 30 and 94% obtained a university degree. Therefore the questionnaire cannot show a proper cross section of the society but is biased towards students.

Furthermore the answers as well as my interpretations might contain different cognitive biases which I will describe next: when interpreting and confirming the hypotheses the possibility of a confirmation bias occurs. A confirmation bias exists whenever "the corroboration of a hypothesis becomes likely" (Oswald & Grosjean, 2004, p. 93). The confirming evidence might have received too much attention while disconfirming details might be disregarded, resulting in an overhasty confirmation of the desired output. In addition the

---

[11] See *2.2 Brand Dimensions*

answers of the questionnaire might also show several biases. The effect of *false memory* can lead to a better or worse image of the evaluated bank. People tend to avoid extreme outputs (*central tendency bias*), therefore many answers are centered around the midpoint of the likert-scale. Garland (1991) points out that participants of a questionnaire tend to give answers in a way to please the interviewer. Relating this aspect to my questionnaire would probably result in a too positive picture of the banks. The *acquiescence bias* supports this idea, indicating that people tend to agree with most of the questions and rather give positive answers (Hurd, 1999). The *social desirability bias* leads to an avoidance of embarrassment. People try to picture themselves in a favorable way (Fisher, 1993). In conclusion the picture of banks given in my questionnaire may be too positive and optimistic. Furthermore the study is built around the banking industry, however, some interpretations are related to the service sector in general.

7.4 Summarizing Conclusions and Outlook

The findings of this study reveal not all predefined brand equity dimensions to possess explanatory power to influence positively brand equity. Only the *hard facts* as brand loyalty and perceived quality in connection with customer satisfaction show a positive and significant effect on brand equity, while brand awareness and brand associations (brand image) do not show explanatory power. As a result banks should place more emphasis directly on the customer and not on the brand itself. The customer and his perceiving of the quality of the bank is the most important thing which is directly related to customer satisfaction and brand loyalty. Therefore every bank should make sure to offer the best possible service quality in order to increase brand equity and ultimately the firm value.

Future research could expand the perspective to other service industries in contrast to product related industries in order to verify the results or show different characteristics for different industries. The dimensions could be updated to obtain a validated and tested list suitable for service related industries. Financial values could be added to the rather qualitative model in order to build a bridge between firm and brand valuation. A financial measurement tool could support either marketing departments or finance departments when evaluating the brand's performance.

8 References

Aaker, D. A. (1991). *Managing Brand Equtiy.* New York.

Aaker, D. A. (1996). Measuring Brand Equity Across Products and Markets. *California Management Review Vol. 38*, pp. 102-120.

Afsar, B., Rehman, Z. U., Qureshi, J. A., & Shahjehan, A. (2010). Determinants of customer loyalty in the banking sector: The case of Pakistan. *African Journal of Business Management Vol.4*, 1040-1047.

Ailawadi, K. L., Lehmann, D. R., & Neslin, S. A. (2003). Revenue Premium as an Outcome Measure of Brand Equity. *Journal of Marketing Vol. 67*, pp. 1-17.

Alba, J. W., Hutchinson, W. J., & Lynch, J. (1991). Memory and Decision Making. In Kassarjian, & Robertson, *Handbook of Consumer Theory and Research* (pp. 1-49). New York.

Anson, W. (2005). *Fundamentals of Intellectual Property Valuation: A Primer for Identifying and Determining Value.* Chicago.

Atilgan, E., Aksoy, S., & Akinci, S. (2005). Determinants of the brand equity: A verification approach in the beverage industry in Turkey. *Marketing Intelligence & Planning Vol. 23*, pp. 237-248.

Bailey, R., & Ball, S. (2006). An exploration of the meanings of hotel brand equity. *The Service Industries Journal Vol. 26*, pp. 15-38.

Barnes, J. G., & Howlett, D. M. (1998). Predictors of equity in relationships between financial services providers and retail customers. *International Journal of Bank Marketing Vol. 16*, 15-23.

Barth, M. E., Clement, M. B., Foster, G., & Kasznik, R. (1998). Brand Values and Capital Market Valuation. *Review of Accounting Studies Vol. 3*, pp. 41-68.

Barwise, P. (1993). Brand equity: Snark or Boojum? *International Journal of Research in Marketing Vol. 10*, pp. 93-104.

Beerli, A., Martín, J. D., & Quintana, A. (2004). A model of customer loyalty in the retail banking market. *European Journal of Marketing Vol. 38*, pp. 253-275.

Bem, D. J. (1987). Writing the empirical journal article. In M. P. Zanna, & J. M. Darley, *The compleat academic: A practical guide for the beginning social scientist* (pp. 171-201). New York.

Berry, L. L. (2000). Cultivating service brand equity. *Academy of Marketing Science Vol. 28*, pp. 128-137.

Blattberg, R. C., & Deighton, J. (1996). Manage Marketing by the Customer Equity Test. *Harvard Business Review Vol. 74*, pp. 133-144.

Brady, M. K., & Cronin, J. J. (2001). Some New Thoughts on Conceptualizing Perceived Service Quality: A Hierarchical Approach. *Journal of Marketing Vol. 65*, pp. 34-49.

Broniarczyk, S. M., & Gershoff, A. D. (2003). The reciprocal effects of brand equity and trivial attributes. *Journal of Marketing Research Vol. 40*, pp. 161-175.

Bruner, G. C., Hensel, P. J., & James, K. E. (2005). *Marketing scales handbook: a compilation of multi-item measures for consumer behavior & advertising.* American Marketing Association.

Campbell, M., & Keller, K. L. (2003). Brand familiarity and ad repetition effects. *Journal of Consumer Research Vol. 30*, pp. 292-304.

Cengiz, E., Ayyildiz, H., & Er, B. (2007). Effects of Image and Advertising Efficiency on Customer Loyalty and Antecedents of Loyalty: Turkish Banks Sample. *Banks and Bank Systems Vol. 2*, pp. 56-83.

Chang, H. H., Hsu, C.-H., & Chung, S. H. (2008). The Antecedents and Consequences of Brand Equity in Service Markets. *Asia Pacific Management Review Vol. 13*, pp. 601-624.

Cronin, J. J., & Taylor, S. A. (1992). Measuring Service Quality: A Reexamination and Extension. *Journal of Marketing Vol. 56*, 55-68.

Dabholkar, P. A., Thorpe, D. I., & Rentz, J. O. (1996). A measure of service quality for retail stores: Scale development and validation. *Journal of the Academy of Marketing Science Vol. 24*, pp. 3-16.

Damodaran, A. (2001). *The Dark Side of Valuation.* New York.

Dhar, R., & Simonson, I. (1992). The effect of the focus of comparison on consumer preferences. *Journal of Marketing Research Vol. 29*, pp. 430-440.

Diener, B. J., & Greyser, S. A. (1978). Consumer Views of Redress Needs. *Journal of Marketing Vol. 42*, 21-27.

Erdem, T., & Swait, J. (1998). Brand Equity as a Signaling Phenomenon. *Journal of Consumer Psychology Vol. 7*, pp. 131-157.

Esch, F.-R. (2003). *Moderne Markenführung: Grundlagen. Innovative Ansätze. Praktische Umsetzungen.* Wiesbaden.

Fama, E. (1970). Efficient Capital Markets: A Review of Theory and Empirical Work. *Journal of Finance Vol. 25*, pp. 383-417.

Ferjani, M., Jedidi, K., & Jagpal, S. (2009). A Conjoint Approach for Consumer- and Firm-Level Brand Valuation. *Journal of Marketing Research Vol. 46*, pp. 846-862.

Fisher, R. J. (1993). Social desirability bias and the validity of indirect questioning. *Journal of Consumer Research Vol. 20*, pp. 303-315.

Foo, M.-H., Douglas, G., & Jack, M. A. (2008). Incentive schemes in the financial services sector. *International Journal of Bank Marketing Vol. 26*, pp. 99-118.

Garland, R. (1991). The Mid-Point on a Rating Scale: Is it Desirable? *Marketing Bulletin Vol. 2*, pp. 66-70.

Goldfarb, A., Lu, Q., & Moorthy, S. (2009). Measuring Brand Value in an Equilibrium Framework. *Marketing Science Vol. 28*, pp. 69-86.

Günther, T., & Kriegbaum, C. (2001). Methoden zur Markenbewertung. *Controlling Vol. 3*, pp. S. 129-137.

Gupta, S., & Zeithaml, V. (2006). Customer Metrics and Their Impact on Financial Performance. *Marketing Science Vol. 6*, pp. 718–739.

Ha, H.-Y., Janda, S., & Muthaly, S. (2010). Development of brand equity: evaluation of four alternative models. *Service Industries Journal Vol. 30*, 911-928.

Hoch, S. J., & Deighton, J. (1989). Managing what consumers learn from experience. *Journal of Marketing Vol. 53*, pp. 1-20.

Hoeffler, S., & Keller, K. L. (2003). The marketing advantages of strong brands. *Brand Management Vol. 10*, pp. 421-445.

Hogan, J. E., Lemon, K. N., & Rust, R. T. (2002). Customer Equity Management. *Journal of Service Research Vol. 5*, pp. 4-12.

Huff, A. S. (1999). *Writing for Scholarly Publication.* Thousand Oaks.

Hurd, M. (1999). Anchoring and Acquiescence Bias in Measuring Assets in Household Surveys . *Journal of Risk and Uncertainty Vol. 19*, pp. 111-136.

Interbrand. (2010). *www.interbrand.com.* Retrieved from http://www.interbrand.com/best_global_brands.aspx

Ivanauskiene, N., & Auruskeviciene, V. (2009). Loyalty Programs Challenges in Retail Banking Industry. *Economics & Management Vol. 14*, pp. 407-412.

Jacoby, J. (1971). A model of multi-brand loyalty. *Journal of Advertising Research*, pp. 25-31.

Kapferer, J.-N. (2008). *The New Strategic Brand Management: Creating and Sustaining Brand Equity.* Philadelphia.

Kayaman, R., & Arasli, H. (2007). Customer based brand equity: evidence from the hotel industry. *Managing Service Quality Vol. 17*, pp. 92-109.

Keiningham, T. L., Aksoy, L., Perkins-Munn, T., & Vavra, T. G. (2005). The Brand-Customer Connection. *Marketing Management Vol. 14*, pp. 33-37.

Keller, K. L. (1993). Conceptualizing, measuring, managing customer-based brand equity. *Journal of Marketing Vol. 57*, pp. 1-22.

Keller, K. L. (1998). *Strategic Brand Managment.* New York.

Keller, K. L. (2008). *Strategic Brand Management: Building, Measuring, and Managing Brand Equity.* New Jersey.

Keller, K. L., & Lehmann, D. R. (2006). Brands and Branding: Research Findings and Future Priorities. *Marketing Science Vol. 25*, pp. 740-759.

Keller, K. L., & Sood, S. (2003). Brand Equity Dilution. *MIT Sloan Management Review*, pp. 12-15.

Kent, R. J., & Allen, C. T. (1994). Competitive interference effects in consumer memory for advertising: The role of brand familiarity. *Journal of Marketing Vol. 58*, pp. 97-105.

Kim, H.-b., Kim, W. G., & An, J. A. (2003). The effect of consumer-based brand equity on firms' financial performance. *Journal of Consumer Marketing Vol. 30*, pp. 335-351.

Kotler, P. (1991). *Marketing Management; Analysis, Planning, Implemetation and Control.* Englewood Cliffs/NJ.

Krishnan, B. C., & Hartline, M. D. (2001). Brand equity: is it more important in services? *Journal of Services Marketing Vol. 15*, pp. 328-342.

Kumar, S. A., Tamilmani, B., Mahalingam, S., & Mani, V. K. (2010). Influence of Service Quality on Attitudinal Loyalty in Private Retail Banking: An Empirical Study. *Journal of Management Research Vol. 9*, pp. 21-38.

Kumar, V., Ramani, G., & Bohling, T. (2004). Customer Lifetime Value Approaches and Best Practice Applications. *Journal of Interactive Marketing Vol. 18*, pp. 60-72.

Lamons, B. (2004). CEO explains need for brand valuation. *Marketing News*, 8-10.

Lehmann, D. R., & Pan, Y. (1994). Context effects, new brand entry, and consideration sets. *Journal of Marketing Research Vol. 31*, pp. 364-374.

Lemon, K. N., Rust, R. T., & Zeithaml, V. A. (2001). What Drives Customer Equity. *Marketing Management Vol. 10*, pp. 1-5.

Leone, R. P., Rao, V. R., Keller, K. L., Luo, A. M., McAlister, L., & Srivastava, R. (2006). Linking Brand Equity to Customer Equity. *Journal of Service Research Vol. 9*, pp. 125-138.

Low, G. S., & Lamb, C. W. (2000). The measurement and dimensionality of brand associations. *Journal of Product and Management Vol. 9*, pp. 350-368.

Mackay, M. M. (2001). Application of brand equity measures in service markets. *Journal of Services Marketing Vol. 15*, pp. 210-221.

Madden, T., Fehle, F., & Fournier, S. (2006). "Brands Matter: An Empirical Demonstration of the Creation of Shareholder Value through Branding. *Journal of the Academy of Marketing Science Vol. 34*, pp. 224–235.

Mahajan, V., Rao, V. R., & Srivastava, R. K. (1994). An Approach to Assess the Importance of Brand Equity in Acquisition Decisions. *Journal of Product Innovation Management Vol. 11*, pp. 221-235.

Malhotra, N. K. (2007). *Marketing Research*. New Jersey.

Markengesetz. (2010). *Markengesetz*. Retrieved from German Trademark Act: http://www.ip-firm.de/markeng_e.pdf

Maul, K.-H., & Mussler, S. (2004). Advanced Brand Valuation. In A. Schimansky, *Der Wert einer Marke* (pp. 60-83). Berlin.

Mellens, M., Dekimpe, M. G., & Steenkamp, J. B. (1996). A review of brand-loyalty measures in marketing. *Tijdschrift voor Economie en Management Vol. 12*, pp. 507-533.

Montgomery, D. B. (1975). New product distribution: An analysis of supermarket buyer decisions. *Journal of Marketing Research Vol. 12*, pp. 255-264.

Motameni, R., & Shahrokhi, M. (1998). Brand equity valuation: a global perspective. *Journal of Product & Management Vol. 7*, pp. 275-290.

Neal, W., & Strauss, R. (2008). *Value Creation: The Power of Brand Equity.* Ohio.

Odin, Y., Odin, N., & Valette-Florence, P. (2001). Conceptual and operational aspects of brand loyalty: An empirical investigation. *Journal of Business Research Vol. 53*, pp. 75-84.

Olivier, R. L. (1999). Whence Consumer Loyalty? *Journal of Marketing Vol. 63*, pp. 33-44.

Oswald, M. E., & Grosjean, S. (2004). Confirmation Bias. In R. F. Pohl, *Cognitive Illusions: A Handbook on Fallacies and Biases in Thinking* (pp. 79-96). Hove.

Parasuraman, A., Zeithaml, V., & Berry, L. (1985). A Conceptual Model of Service Quality and Its Implications for Future Research. *Journal of Marketing Vol. 49*, pp. 41-50.

Richins, M. L. (1983). Negative word-of-mouth by dissatisfied consumers: A pilot study. *Journal of Marketing Vol. 47*, 68-78.

Rundle-Thiele, S., & Bennet, R. (2001). A brand for all seasons? A discussion of brand loyalty approaches and their applicability for different markets. *Journal of Product and Brand Management Vol. 10*, pp. 25-37.

Rust, R. T., Ambler, T., Carpenter, G. S., Kumar, V., & Srivastava, R. K. (2004). Measuring Marketing Productivity: Current Knowledge and Future Directions. *Journal of Marketing Vol. 68*, pp. 76-89.

Rust, R. T., Lemon, K. N., & Zeithaml, V. A. (2004). Return on Marketing: Using Customer Equity to Focus Marketing Strategy. *Journal of Marketing Vol. 68*, pp. 109-127.

Salinas, G., & Ambler, T. (2009). A taxonomy of brand valuation practice: Methodologies and purposes. *Brand Management Vol. 17*, pp. 39–61.

Sander, M. (1994). *Die Bestimmung und Steuerung des Wertes von Marken (Dissertation).* Heidelberg.

Sattler, H. (2005). *Markenbewertung: State of the Art.* Retrieved from Universität Hamburg: http://www.uni-hamburg.de/fachbereiche-einrichtungen/fb03/ihm/rp27.pdf

Sattler, H., & Völckner, F. (2007). *Markenpolitik.* Stuttgart.

Sattler, H., Högl, S., & Hupp, O. (2002). Evaluation of the Financial Value of Brands. *Research Papers on Marketing and Retailing (University of Hamburg).*

Schimanski, A. (2004). *Der Wert der Marke: Markenbewertungsverfahren für ein erfolgreiches Markenmanagement.* Berlin.

Sethuraman, R., & Cole, C. (1997). Why Do Consumers Pay More for National Brands than for Store Brands. *Marketing Science Institute*, pp. 97-126.

Siddiqi, K. O. (2011). Interrelations between Service Quality Attributes, Customer Satisfaction and Customer Loyalty in the Retail Banking Sector in Bangladesh. *International Journal of Business and Management Vol. 6*, pp. 12-36.

Simon, C. J., & Sullivan, M. W. (1993). The Measurement and Determinants of Brand Equity: A Financial Approach. *Marketing Science Vol. 12*, pp. 28-53.

Simon, H. (1979). Dynamics of price elasticity and brand life cycles: An empirical study. *Journal of Marketing Research Vol. 16*, pp. 439-452.

Sirgy, J., Lee, D. J., Johar, J. S., & Tidwell, J. (2008). Effect of self-congruity with sponsorship on brand loyalty. *Journal of Business Research Vol. 61*, pp. 1091-1097.

Sivakumar, K., & Raj, S. P. (1997). Quality tier competition: How price change influences brand choice and category choice. *Journal of Marketing Vol. 61*, pp. 71-84.

Srinivasan, S., & Hanssens, D. M. (2009). Marketing and Firm Value. *Journal of Marketing Research Vol. 46*, pp. 293-312.

Sun, L., & Ghiselli, R. F. (2010). Developing a Conceptual Model of Brand Equity in the Hotel Industry Based on Aaker's Perspective. *Journal of Quality Assurance in Hospitality & Tourism Vol. 11*, pp. 147-161.

Tabachnik, B. G., & Fidell, L. S. (2007). *Using multivariate statistics.* Boston.

Tolba, A. H., & Hassan, S. S. (2009). Linking customer-based brand equity with brand market performance: a managerial approach. *Journal of Product & Brand Management Vol. 18*, 356-366.

Tong, X., & Hawley, J. M. (2009). Measuring customer-based brand equity: Empirical evidence from the sportswear market in China. *Journal of Product & Brand Management Vol. 18*, pp. 262-271.

Trommsdorff, V. (2004). Verfahren der Markenbewertung. In *Handbuch Markenführung* (pp. 1856-1875).

Turley, L. W., & Moore, P. A. (1995). Brand name strategies in the service sector. *Journal of Consumer Marketing Vol. 12*, pp. 42-50.

Vargo, S. L., & Lusch, R. F. (2008). Service-dominant logic: continuing the evolution. *Journal of the Academy of Marketing Science Vol. 36*, pp. 1-10.

Wood, L. (2000). Brands and brand equity: definition and management. *Management Decision Vol. 38*, pp. 662-669.

Wyner, G. (2001). The Trouble With Brand Equity Valuation. *Marketing Research Vol. 13*, pp. 4-5.

Yoo, B., Donthu, N., & Lee, S. (2000). An Examination of Selected Marketing Mix Elements and Brand Equity. *Journal of the Academy of Marketing Science Vol. 28*, pp. 195-211.

Zeithaml, V. (1988). Consumer perceptions of price, quality, and value: a means-end and synthesis of evidence. *Journal of Marketing Vol. 52*, pp. 2-22.

9 Appendix

Questionnaire

Bank is defined in this context as the financial institution, the participant usually goes to in order to carry out all his financial concerns.

Gender:

Male   Female

Age:

Under 30 years   Over 30 years

Educational background:

Have you obtained a degree from higher education?

(university/university of applied science)?

Yes   No

I do not like to change to another bank because I value the selected bank.

        1   2   3   4   5   6   7

Strongly disagree   Strongly agree

I am a loyal customer to my bank.

        1   2   3   4   5   6   7

Strongly disagree   Strongly agree

I would always recommend my bank to someone who seeks my advice.

        1   2   3   4   5   6   7

Strongly disagree   Strongly agree

To what extent does this bank live up to your general expectations of it?

1   2   3   4   5   6   7

Not at all   To full extent

Imagine the perfect bank. How far and/or close does this bank come to your ideal?

1   2   3   4   5   6   7

Not at all   To full ideal

Given your experience with this bank, how satisfied or dissatisfied are you with it overall?

1   2   3   4   5   6   7

Dissatisfied   Satisfied

My bank is of high quality.

1   2   3   4   5   6   7

Strongly disagree   Strongly agree

The likely quality of my bank is extremely high.

1   2   3   4   5   6   7

Strongly disagree   Strongly agree

The likelihood that my bank would be functional is very high.

1   2   3   4   5   6   7

Strongly disagree   Strongly agree

The likelihood that my bank is reliable is very high.

1   2   3   4   5   6   7

Strongly disagree   Strongly agree

My bank must be of very good quality.

1   2   3   4   5   6   7

Strongly disagree   Strongly agree

My bank appears to be of very poor quality.

1   2   3   4   5   6   7

Strongly disagree   Strongly agree

I would say that my bank's physical environment is one of the best in its industry.

1   2   3   4   5   6   7

Strongly disagree   Strongly agree

I would rate my bank's physical environment highly.

1   2   3   4   5   6   7

Strongly disagree   Strongly agree

I would say that my bank provides superior service.

1   2   3   4   5   6   7

Strongly disagree   Strongly agree

I believe my bank offers excellent service.

1   2   3   4   5   6   7

Strongly disagree   Strongly agree

I know what my bank (logo) looks like.

1   2   3   4   5   6   7

Strongly disagree   Strongly agree

I can recognize my bank among other competing brands.

1   2   3   4   5   6   7

Strongly disagree   Strongly agree

I am aware of my bank (logo).

1   2   3   4   5   6   7

Strongly disagree   Strongly agree

Some characteristics of my bank come to my mind quickly.

1   2   3   4   5   6   7

Strongly disagree   Strongly agree

I can quickly recall the symbol or logo of my bank.

1   2   3   4   5   6   7

Strongly disagree   Strongly agree

I have difficulty in imagining my bank (logo) in my mind.

1   2   3   4   5   6   7

Strongly disagree   Strongly agree

It makes sense to buy products/services of my bank instead of any other brand, even if they are the same.

1 2 3 4 5 6 7

Strongly disagree   Strongly agree

Even if another brand has same features as my bank, I would prefer to buy at my bank.

1 2 3 4 5 6 7

Strongly disagree   Strongly agree

If there is another brand as good as my bank, I prefer to buy from my bank.

1 2 3 4 5 6 7

Strongly disagree   Strongly agree

If another brand is not different from my bank in any way, it seems smarter to purchase from my bank.

1 2 3 4 5 6 7

Strongly disagree   Strongly agree

Table 17: Cronbachs Alpha

Item-Total Statistics

	Scale Mean if Item Deleted	Scale Variance if Item Deleted	Corrected Item-Total Correlation	Cronbach's Alpha if Item Deleted
LO1	133,44	231,608	,703	,913
LO2	133,35	233,969	,616	,915
LO3	133,36	230,312	,709	,913
CS1	133,66	235,046	,705	,914
CS2	134,08	234,354	,610	,915
CS3	133,16	232,795	,714	,914
PQ1	133,29	232,447	,790	,913
PQ2	133,37	232,114	,759	,913
PQ3	133,21	234,406	,687	,914
PQ4	132,95	239,248	,587	,916
PQ5	133,15	238,128	,603	,915
PQ6_reversed	132,86	237,341	,556	,916
SQ1	134,22	238,492	,432	,918
SQ2	134,07	238,505	,451	,918
SQ3	133,62	233,857	,716	,914
SQ4	133,94	230,436	,708	,913
AW1	132,64	243,052	,372	,919
AW2	132,84	240,735	,322	,920
AW3	132,67	241,662	,379	,919
AS1	133,06	240,876	,395	,918
AS2	132,73	243,218	,303	,920
AS3_reversed	132,79	242,746	,225	,923
BE1	134,21	235,466	,445	,918
BE2	133,83	229,341	,616	,915
BE3	133,81	231,874	,590	,915
BE4	134,50	239,572	,306	,921

Figure 5: Histogram

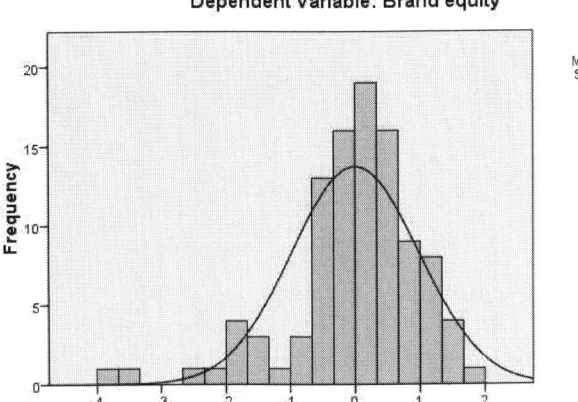

Dependent Variable: Brand equity

Figure 6: P-P plot

Normal P-P Plot of Regression Standardized Residual

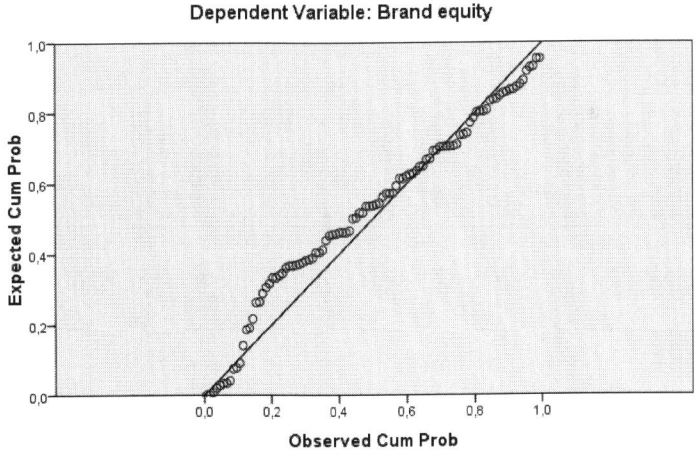

Dependent Variable: Brand equity

Printed in Great Britain
by Amazon.co.uk, Ltd.,
Marston Gate.